LOVE DRONES

LOVE DRONES

NOAM DORR

SARABANDE BOOKS
Louisville, KY

Library of Congress Cataloging-in-Publication Data

Names: Dorr, Noam, author.

Title: Love drones : essays / Noam Dorr.

Description: First edition. | Louisville, KY : Sarabande Books, 2019

Identifiers: LCCN 2018051456 (print) | LCCN 2018058006 (e-book)

ISBN 9781946448392 (e-book) | ISBN 9781946448385 (alk. paper)

Classification: LCC PS3604.O768 (e-book) | LCC PS3604.O768 A6 2019 (print)

DDC 814/.6—dc23

LC record available at https://lccn.loc.gov/2018051456

Cover art by Cody Coppernoll.

Cover and interior design by Alban Fischer.

Manufactured in Canada.

This book is printed on acid-free paper.

Sarabande Books is a nonprofit literary organization.

This project is supported in part by the National Endowment for the Arts.
The Kentucky Arts Council, the state arts agency, supports Sarabande Books with
state tax dollars and federal funding from the National Endowment for the Arts.

One might just as well try this: When something explodes,
Turn exactly opposite from it and see what there is to see.

The loud will take care of itself, and everyone will be able to say
What happened in that direction. But who is looking

The other way?

—ALBERTO RÍOS

To extract each fragment by each fragment from the word from the image another
word another image the reply that will not repeat history in oblivion.

—THERESA HAK KYUNG CHA

The secrets we choose to betray lose power over us.

—LOUISE GLÜCK

CONTENTS

Navigate by feel until the eyes adjust—let the aperture of the pupil open. To walk into my father's darkroom means walking away from the calls of crows and mourning doves in the pines, from an uncontainable saturation of sun—sun from above, sun reflecting off the sand below—through the worn-down wood door of the shack that used to be part of the kibbutz children's home. Six children slept in this room once. Past the light and past the curtain and into a dripping black. Then dark dissolves into low red, and water flows off the bodies hanging from the wires.

For pinhole cameras; Don't try to photograph indoors while making your first image—inside exposures can be long and difficult to estimate. Don't let the sun shine directly on the pinhole when exposing. Don't photograph into deep shade. Don't hold the camera in your hand. Set the camera on a wall, the ground, or on another solid base. Steady the camera with a weight if it's windy. Photograph where there is brightness, partial shade, and shadow all in the same image.

LOVE DRONES

We are star struck on the edge. A drone operator walks out of an Air Force trailer in a desert and smokes a cigarette. The Predator drone looks like a blind whale—the front of the aircraft has a hump, so it is a whale, and my mind attempts to turn everything into a face, and this face has no eyes, so it is blind, but nonetheless its sensors are better than my eyes, or at least, can see what I can never see, delve into other spectra. The drone operator does not see the Predator itself, the predator himself, the Predator is in Afghanistan, the operator in Nevada. We are stars struck on the edge. The difference between my sight and the drone's is even worse than most, because I am colorblind, and so the camera feed from the drone would never even translate into the right sight. While the rifle's sight is on the target, a cardboard cutout of a man with a yellow bull's-eye where his throat would be, the sergeant at the firing range says look for that yellow halo, then pull the trigger of your M-16; aim too low and the halo becomes a dot, aim too high and it disappears altogether—and all day at the firing range it is my search for that yellow halo. Perhaps love is only a hindrance for pulling the trigger on a joystick and launching a Hellfire missile from the wing of a Predator drone, but certainly hate is also not a necessity, nor soon will be touch: engineers are working on vocal launch commands, and after that brain waves. The star's edge strikes us. The drone operator drives to his house in the outskirts of Las Vegas, and through the vantage point of his windshield he sees the casino replicas of the Statue of Liberty, the Eiffel Tower, the Great Pyramid of Giza. The star's edge strokes us. What of desire? The operator is not a lover, but like a lover, reaches for the target, searches on the screen under other spectra for his object. It is easy to place trailers with humans in one desert to connect via satellite to drones in another desert—there is plenty of room in deserts and plenty of room in the sky. Stars suspended strike. In the crook of the drone operator's finger there was a drop of sweat, right before he pulled the trigger; it is labor after all. Is there no desire in the striking of stars, do they extend out of their own internal reactions? It is easy to fake monuments in the desert emptiness, to create a text with no context. In the desert the operator's fatigues blend with the sand and in the suburbs his polo shirt blends with the lawn and he disappears for us. Unmanned, we seem to desert our desire. If I had a drone I would point it to the moon to see how far it would go, not too far before the air becomes too thin, I know.

The drone of a sustained musical note creating a harmonic effect throughout a musical piece; bagpipes drone and sitars too—put your cheek against the instrument and it will hum in your teeth, but I prefer the synth loops of Suicide's "Dream Baby Dream," that mechanical haunting from the year of my birth. A crossroads is just a place where our decisions are based on preexisting infrastructure; instead of taking one road or another we could just choose to walk off into the unpaved dirt. Mostly though, we don't. Futurists like Ray Kurzweil think we are on the cusp of a singularity—the arrival in the near future of a technological shift so drastic we cannot possibly comprehend the resulting new reality. He is considered to be an optimist. We stroke the star's edge. After the firing range we take the bus back to the base, to intelligence headquarters, and the rifle remains a heavy burden as I lean against the glass; I do not want the bus to pause at a crossroads' red light, I want the humming of the struggling engine to drown out the rest and for the pistons to never stop. A singularity may prove to be a crisis, a crisis from Greek *krisis*, a decision, a crisis as in a crossroads. The drones have their own avian beauty; in the same way baby birds are hideous to me, yet their translucent skin compels their parents to care. We edge along the star's stroke. Suicide sings "Dream baby dream / Keep those dreams burning forever / Forever and ever," and I want to close my eyes and disappear into the imagined pauses in the hum. Kurzweil says technological growth is exponential, that human technological capacity has been doubling itself every ten years or so throughout human existence, which for a medieval peasant isn't so dramatic, perhaps a new development once or twice in a lifetime—the introduction of the horse collar to better break the surface of the earth, or the chimney to slip smoke out of our eyes—but for us in the twenty-first century means experiencing the equivalent of the previous twenty thousand years of human development in just the span of our short lives. The striking edge stars us. Human weeping can be a drone, but not laughter—which is in its essence the cutting of sound in and out, in and out. We are on edge for striking stars. Experts say the next technological revolution, especially in war, will be robotics; science fiction has been saying so for quite some time, but we are now seeing drones patrol the skies and robotic vehicles with machine guns for arms accompany marines on their tours of duty. Stand still on the star's edge. The drone of heavy machinery immediately puts me at ease—as an asthmatic child exertion turns into breathlessness, excitement into paralysis, so I sit there slowly sucking on the vapors from the nebulizer, my ears filled with vibration rumblings, until finally my airway expands.

Weeping, machine buzz, the ramblings of the person sitting behind us on the bus whom we have no desire to listen to—what is a drone but the repetition over and over of that which we wish our understanding to cut through? Stricken by stars or awe struck, or are we awaiting a strike, the blow to cut through the droning, on the edge? Predator drones are employed in an asymmetrical struggle, the most refined technology of war in opposition to the crudest, though the rusty nails and scrap metal explosions of IEDs and suicide bombers do contain a symmetry—the extension of all motion from a central point, like the combustion of a star. Perhaps the noise can drain into a hiding place for violence, a container we can't tap into, or, more likely, are too bored to care to search for. The marine stationed in Afghanistan says he loves the buzzing sound of a Predator drone; it means he is safe. Turning off the nebulizer should be a relief, a signal that the treatment is over and the airways open again, but there is always a loneliness in the absolute absence of that sound and vibration. There are skeptics of the singularity, so-called pessimists, who see the present and say vehicles are not moving faster, dishwashers and refrigerators and ovens are not making household work easier, and life spans are not extending drastically longer than they were forty years ago. Or does the edge strain into a drop, a star's strength drain into a drone? Predators themselves are not as refined as they may seem—their four-cylinder engines not much different than those of snowmobiles. Even the Hellfire is over thirty years old. And so the newness of Predators is not in their bodies but in the ideas that govern their use. For stars striking, so distant from one another, are light and touch the same? Back at the base the M-16s are returned to the weapons' shed, a load heavier than the rifle's weight lifts, and I return to search the computer screen, my sight set elsewhere, translating the information for our next target. Weeping for the striking of stars. While for Afghans in the same geography the droning of Predators translates into—time to run. We stars striking at the edges waiting for them to meet. After running breathlessness was painful, as was getting monthly allergy shots, and when the pain became too great I cried and tears spliced light which became stars in my eyes.

They want to use the photo in a press
conference. They want to show ambulances are
not to be trusted. Hospitals are not to trusted.
Kindergartens are not to be trusted. They say
the images taken from the drone clearly reveal
the operative taking a rocket launcher out of
the back of an ambulance. *Here,* they say, *here
is the evidence of wrongdoing, that we cannot
trust them.* And there are precedents. Still, I
think it looks like a pole, perhaps a rolled-up
stretcher. They—we—bombed the town just
a few minutes before, so who is to know if the
human figure moving below is out to harm or
to recover from harm.

A STUDY IN THREE ORANGES

Act so that there is no use in a centre.

—GERTRUDE STEIN

THE ORANGE SWEETNESS OF MARCH

There is a point around March when the sweetness of citrus blossoms covers the valley—covers up all of the smells of the everyday: the shit from the cow pens, the rotting orange peels turning into cattle feed, the burnt turkey feathers and bones outside the slaughterhouse. For about a week the kibbutz is perfumed in just the right way—you step outside, inhale deeply, and all of your senses reach out with desire.

THE ENGINEER, SEGMENT I

The two men were sentenced to death for their involvement with the Jewish underground. The Engineer was given a challenge: the two men wanted to commit suicide before the British military hanged them. If they were to die, they said, let it be by their own hands while taking the lives of as many occupiers as possible. The Engineer had a problem: how to smuggle explosives from his jail cell to their jail cell.

THE ORANGE SURRENDERS

No one I know eats an orange whole, bites into the sphere like an apple. One eats oranges by fragmenting. The orange yields itself to breaking. In many parts we can share the fruit with others, or appreciate the moment between each segment. Or else we drink the orange up as juice, forgetting we are drinking many oranges—each sip a collective of individual fruits, a collective of individual trees.

The Inventor sees himself as an intellectual farmer. By day he toils in the kibbutz orchards, sees the oranges carried to the factory. By night he sits at his bench and dreams of efficiency. He dreams of an office in the middle of the orchard with a computer and sensors and *office conditions*. He is haunted by a desire for the perfection of oranges—an orchard-complex with definite input and output—each tree measured and precisely watered using drip irrigation. He dreams of an invention that will make this efficiency possible.

VALLEY ORANGE

There were two factories in the kibbutz—one aboveground and one below. The juice factory where I worked, where my sister and father and grandfather worked, was built in 1940 because the kibbutz could not make enough money to sustain itself and there was an increasing demand by the British military stationed in Palestine for canned goods during the Second World War. The explosives factory was built in the bottom of a well in the fields outside the kibbutz. While the factory above nourished the occupiers, the factory below was meant to expel them. The explosives would also be used in the war to come with the Arab neighbors over this land. My grandfather served as a liaison between the kibbutz members and the explosive manufacturers. My father says he still remembers British soldiers in the valley. Kalaniot *we called them*, he says, *anemones*, because their red berets were the same color as the flower—a red sphere on a green background. The anemones besieged the kibbutz in 1945, searching for illegal arms and people, though as a result of the deaths they caused they ended their search early and found neither. Anemones bloom after the winter rains, right before the oranges. In the valley oranges grow on a green background. The only anemones left now are the actual flowers.

THE WATCHMAKER, SEGMENT I

The audience watches the orange tree—it is only a potted plant the height of a child on a stage, nothing special about the thin trunk here. Then leaves begin to shift slightly. White flowers emerge. Full oranges burst through a screen of green, oranges at the peak of ripeness, oranges picked from the tree, oranges cut into sections and fed to the audience who taste how real and sweet they are. The audience could have attempted to watch this unfold in an orchard over a season, and would have failed—the eye incapable of perceiving movement so slight, humans incapable of living in botanical time. Here the Watchmaker sees the audience watching as the life of a plant is revealed. When the juice hits their tongue how can they deny that they and the orange were moving at the same pace?

THE ORANGE IN HUMAN FORM

My sister is dancing in a circle with a papier-mâché orange on her head. The orange is so large it functions like a helmet. It is bright orange, more orange than an orange, and includes a green stem and leaf. All of the second graders are participating in this dance. They're wearing white, which is the color one wears for Shavuot. Their bodies disappear, which makes the orange more orange. The oranges that are their heads are floating in that circle while the community watches. Shavuot is my favorite holiday because we eat cheesecake; it is my favorite because all of the kibbutz *anafim*—*anaf* like the branch of a tree, but also of industry—gather in the emptied horse track and we have a parade. Each anaf decorates a tractor and turns it into a float to represent production for the year. The last float to pass is a tractor pulling a train of tiny cars—each car occupied by parents holding a child born that year. Once the avocado anaf used its three-wheeled fruit-pickers to choreograph a dance; each driver stood on a platform at the top of the long hydraulic neck, high above the crowd. Circling each other to the tune of *The Blue Danube* they looked like the most elegant mechanized giraffes.

THE ENGINEER, SEGMENT II

The Engineer describes the moment when the idea comes to him: eight oranges in a metal bowl, a dessert at the end of their meal, arriving to the table he shares with seven other inmates. There is a joy of invention that comes from breaking down a problem into its component parts. *The oranges spoke to me,* he says. They became desire. Two grenades were smuggled to the men in the form of hollowed-out oranges filled with explosives and shrapnel. Before the execution they embraced each other—held one of the oranges between their chests, detonated it with their final cigarette—and killed only themselves. There were oranges in the bowl because it was the month of April. In April you see the full span of a tree, the entire growing season. Across an orchard, bud to fruit overlap. The air is sweet.

THE ORANGE IN POMEGRANATES

The word for grenade in Hebrew, *rimon,* is the same as the word for pomegranate. Not unlike how pomegranate's English etymology stems from the Spanish *granada*—this fruit with a crown and many seeds, this fruit like a grenade's fuse and filler. When museums in Israel and military history sites talk about the two men who committed suicide, the name given to this story in Hebrew is *rimon bein halevavot*, which can be translated as both *grenade between the hearts* and *pomegranate between the hearts*. Though as I mentioned, the fruit they used was an orange.

ORANGES IN THE SEASONS

When we are told the story of the Engineer and his orange grenades the oranges are already there, in the bowl, in the cell, in the Jerusalem prison. It is April, therefore it is orange season. What we do not know is where the oranges came from. How they arrived to the table. Whose hands planted the trees, watered the roots, trimmed the branches, picked the fruit, wrapped it and crated it and shipped it. Since the Engineer is on the inside of the prison, since he could not leave to buy the oranges, it is very likely that he does not know where they came from either. They could have come from the Engineer's parents' orchard—they were citrus growers—or they could have come from the valley where I'm from. One thing we do know: the oranges did not come from Jerusalem. Oranges do not grow on those hills.

THE INVENTOR, SEGMENT II

The factory opened and oranges became a way of life. The Inventor was surrounded by them. Blossoms in February. Fruit in March. Rotting silage by June. Nothing was wasted—the squeezed-out fruit left to ferment as feed for the cows. There was an efficiency to the order of things, but it was not the same as monitoring every tree from an office.

From the time the British controlled this land the juice factory became the main source of income for the kibbutz. We ate the fruit right after it was picked in the orchard and drank juice from the carton when it came out of the factory. So many of the community have gone through the factory's assembly lines, everyone working at least one shift at some point. As children we played among discarded factory parts—hiding inside empty steel drums meant for concentrate, building towers out of plastic syrup bottles, rolling on giant aseptic foil bags pretending they were waterbeds. Slowly, several shares at a time, the juice factory was sold to Coca-Cola, until the workers were replaced by people from the city and the gates were closed to us.

SACRIFICIAL ORANGE

People now call the story *Rimon between the Hearts*, but at the time the underground called it *Operation May I Die with The Philistines*. "May I Die with the Philistines" is a common phrase expressing sacrifice and heroism, recalling the story of Samson—blinded, and chained to two columns, Samson brought down the Philistine temple on his enemies and on himself. I knew it well enough at five, that when I was playing at my friend's house and my parents made me give her back the golden keychain she said I could have, I got so angry that I stretched my hands across the doorframe in the hallway and pushed as hard as I could to bring the house down on all of us, thinking but not saying: *May I Die with the Philistines!*

The magical orange tree flowered throughout the year no matter the season. Some records show the Watchmaker's oranges were made of silk. Or the branches were of silk. Or sometimes the leaves. At least some of the fruits were real, real enough to be offered to the audience to taste. Of course, for the tree to appear alive on any day, at any time, the plant had to be completely dead, its organic functions replaced by an intricate automaton.

ARRANGED ORANGE

The word for orange in Hebrew, *tapuz*, is an amalgamation of two: *tapu'akh* meaning "apple" and *zahav* meaning "gold." But "tapuz between the hearts" with all of its explosive consonants sounds ridiculous.

AN ORANGE TRICK

I'd like to say that I'm the kind of person who learned from his grand-father how to peel an orange in one long spiraling strip. That he would take a fine-edged knife, place the point against the rind, and turn until it unraveled, exposing the sphere beneath. There is no usefulness in this continuous gold, it is only testament to a skill. The truth is: when he and I approached a citrus fruit we would use our bare hands, look for any weak point to begin, and tear at the rind piece by piece.

He told his superior, another inmate, that his plan was to smuggle the grenades as oranges. His superior told his superior who told the underground. At first his plan was rejected; it was too fanciful. And years later, in an interview, he still seems bothered that they ever doubted his ability. For him it was a craftsman's assignment, an engineer's meditation. For him it was the wonder of discovery. The death of the two men was secondary.

INVERTED ORANGE

The Engineer had already been in the prison for four years when the leaders of the underground came to him to design the oranges. He was only twenty-three, but the two men sentenced to death were even younger. The prison was also twenty-three years old when the two men detonated the orange. That part of Jerusalem, the Russian Compound, had seen many iterations. Before it was a British prison the building was a women's hostel for Russian pilgrims visiting the holy sites. Before that, it was an Ottoman military parade ground. Before that, a Roman military base. Before that, an Assyrian garrison.

AN ORANGE STING

An occupied space creates layers where you peel back one surface and another reveals itself. Peel back an orange and what you get are segments. When we ran away laughing from the children's home we would go to the orchards outside the kibbutz fence to pick and peel the fruit. Before our fingers broke apart the sections, we made a game of sticking our thumbs through the space in the center of an orange or a clementine or a grapefruit. We would pretend our thumbs and the fruit were one organ, stung by an insect and swollen. A clementine was the sting of a bee and an orange of a wasp.

A DEBT OF ORANGE

At the end of a shift, when I return home from the factory with orange pulp in my hair and orange concentrate covering my shoes, it's hard to think of the fruit as precious. Oranges are so abundant in the kibbutz they hardly have any value; it's hard to find worth in an object you see rotting every day. Still, oranges *are* valuable. They were valuable to the Palestinians here before the factory was even built. What amazes me most about the story of the two men who committed suicide is the story of the Russian Compound. When the British departed Palestine in 1948, the newly established State of Israel took over the lot—the police station where the two men detonated the orange is still there, used for the same purpose under an Israeli flag. The Soviet Union, which technically owned the land, pressured the Israeli government to pay for it. The Israeli government, strapped for foreign currency, was unable to pay the entire price tag, so an agreement was reached: under the Orange Treaty thousands of tons of oranges were shipped to the Soviet Union until one-third of the remaining debt was paid. I am amazed that the place where the orange grenades were made and unmade was later bought with oranges.

THE INVENTOR, SEGMENT III

The idea came to him as he was pruning. He noticed two branches from two different trees on the ground. One was green-leafed and bursting with fruit, the other brown and dead. It struck him that the leaf represented the tree, and if the leaf had enough water so did the entire plant. If only there was a way to measure one in order to know the other.

VALLEY ORANGE

British soldiers raided the kibbutz after members of the Jewish underground blew up a coastal radar station. The British were using the radar to locate boats carrying Jewish World War II refugees. Using guide dogs, the British military tracked the saboteurs to my kibbutz as the point of origin.

WHEN THE CARGO IS NOT AN ORANGE

The refugees arriving by boats in the night were called *ma'apilim*, those who reach a higher plane. Since they exceeded the Jewish quota the British set for entering Palestine, they were considered illegal. Packed together in ships too small, they reached the beach not too far from the kibbutz where members of the Jewish underground would collect, then scatter them across different kibbutzim and villages so the British could not find them. When the oranges were shipped out of Palestine, they were first individually hand-wrapped, then carefully packaged. Precious cargo—especially for Europeans, especially for the British—they were collected into crates and scattered across the world.

The British military surrounded the kibbutz and began searching for the men who blew up the radar station. A call came through for Jews in the area to break the siege and scatter among the residents to make it impossible for the British to identify the saboteurs hiding inside. Unarmed, facing thousands of anemones, the leaders of the group waiting outside the kibbutz hesitated to approach the armed line. In the field between the factory and the orchards where they gathered, one woman stood and cried *Forward for the homeland!* and rushed the line. The rest followed. She reached the British soldiers first and was shot twelve times. She was the same age as the two men who committed suicide. Her name is not inscribed on a monument, a mannequin showing her midstride with hundreds following is not displayed in a museum, her story was not written. When the dust settled, eight of the group, including her, were dead and dozens wounded. Both sides stopped the confrontation to provide first aid. As the British moved between the bodies, the anemones asked, *Why are you unarmed? Why are your arms empty?*

THE WATCHMAKER, SEGMENT III

Magic opened to him by accident—when he was an apprentice watchmaker an absentminded bookshop clerk gave him two treatises on magic instead of the watchmaker's manuals he asked for. That first night he was so consumed by the world opening to him that when his lamp ran out of oil he decided to steal the town's streetlight and bring it back to his bedroom to continue reading. We don't know whether those books contained the tricks that became his marvelous orange tree. We do know that it was this desire for mystery that brought the tree alive.

GLOBAL ORANGE

An orange circulates. Try to point to the origin of the desire for citrus and your finger will keep sliding across the map. Jews introduced citrus to Europe through the citron. Berbers from North Africa brought the orange tree to southern Spain. The orange was reintroduced to the Middle East by Portuguese merchants, hence its Arabic name, *bortukal*. Crusaders brought the orange blossom back to Europe where it became a symbol of fruitfulness worn at weddings. "To gather orange blossoms" meant to seek a wife. And in England after Queen Victoria wore a wreath of them at her wedding demand grew so high that a class divide became apparent between those who could afford real as opposed to wax blossoms. All citrus originally came from Southeast Asia. An orange circulates.

THE ORANGE AND THE POMEGRANATE

Neither pomegranate nor orange are particularly beautiful trees. More like shrubs really. Something about their appearance escapes definition. A row of citrus trees will bleed into one another until they become a mass of green dotted with orange. A pomegranate tree feels like a mere extension of the greenery around it, like an upright lawn. Nothing about these trees is distinctive. Orange blossoms, however, are sharp pointed stars, each stamen calling out its singularity, calling to the bees to propagate it. And the flower of a pomegranate as it transforms into its fruit is a red profusion—like a freeze-frame photo of an exploding heart.

THE ENGINEER, SEGMENT IV

In the interview the Engineer is proudest of new evidence that emerged fifty years later. It proved he was accurate about the sequence of events, that the story unfolded just as he analyzed at the time, that he was able to break down the narrative into its component parts. He is a thin-boned-looking man, sitting upright on a sofa. Behind him are cushions embroidered with the Eiffel Tower, a cup of café au lait, French phrases. The man who made the orange into a machine heard but did not see the result of his work. *I heard one explosion, and another. I knew they must have detonated.*

A CHRONOLOGY OF ORANGE

They say that the plan was for the two men to use one orange on themselves, and the other to kill the British officers escorting them to the gallows. They say the two men were torn about using the second orange because it turned out that the prison rabbi would be accompanying their execution party. In the end they chose to use only one. Even though this story is enshrined as true no one knows the last thoughts and conversations of two men right before they take their own lives. No one tells us what happened to the second orange.

A FAILURE OF ORANGE

I try to recreate the Engineer's oranges for a writing workshop. My oranges are not filled with explosives and shrapnel, but strips of paper, one for each line in this essay. I go to three grocery stores in the city in the state in the country where I now live, but the oranges are all wrong. The Engineer definitively says in his interview that he used a Shamouti orange. Shamoutis, developed in the nineteenth century by Palestinian farmers, are oval and sweet with hardly any seeds and their rinds are thick. But in this city there are no Shamouti oranges. In each store I hold the fruit and imagine it arriving to the Engineer in a silver bowl, ready for mechanizing. Though navels are the most common, their skin is thin and fragile. Tangerines are too small and would hardly contain all of the text without bursting open. Blood oranges come closest, their peel a little thicker, but their color is not orange. Defeated, I go with the fragile navels. I try to maintain fidelity to the Engineer's methods: I carefully slice off the top of the orange with a razor, scoop out the pulp with a spoon, attach the top back on with toothpicks (he used splinters from the underside of his workbench). But the navels' skin is too thin, I can't prevent the seams from showing. These oranges are all wrong.

VALLEY ORANGE

According to a farmer in the valley I am from, it is the Shamouti's ability to root deep in our sandy soil that allows it to succeed there. And this is true. The valley looks lush now, but if you scrape the top layer off you will find that everything here is built on a stretch of sand.

BORING ORANGE

At a party I tell some friends excitedly about my research, the story of the Engineer and how he created these orange bombs, the story of the two men. But the conversation slides off the topic. There is no space in this room, in a country so far from the orchards, for this kind of story. Not like I'm invisible, but more like I'm obsessed with a strange detail, a random fragment of history that bears no relevance or interest to anyone anymore.

The Inventor was faced with a problem: How can the center know when a plant needs watering? He built a sensor that detects the fluctuations in the firmness of a leaf. If the leaf was dry and limp, so too the tree. The sensor was connected to a recorder, the recorder to a computer, and the computer to an irrigation valve. A slight decrease in a leaf's fullness, and water would rush to its aid. In the early stages, when the Inventor was working on the prototype, the data from each sensor was transferred to old cassette recorders. The Inventor would walk from tree to tree, hit Eject, collect each tape. To passersby it would appear as though he had recorded the trees speaking, as if he was interviewing them, searching for their story.

A FAILURE OF ORANGE

In first grade I imagined myself an inventor and took on the mission to refine our weapons of war. In our struggle against the second graders I knew there were better tools than balls of mud. And so came the idea for balls of mud with acorns in the center to increase pain, mirrors to reflect the sun and scorch the older children, trapdoors of bamboo over deep pits to trap them. I only ever got as far as the initial idea. I never followed through.

INSIDE THE ORANGE MACHINE

The limit of the eight-hour factory shift is the limit of gestures in space and time. Four workers run the line: Position One loads the empty bottles. Position Two fastens the caps. Position Three places the bottles in the boxes. Position Four stacks the boxes on the pallets.

I liked Position Four best because it allowed for the greatest elasticity of time—if I stacked the boxes in fast bursts I could create a space of five or six seconds where I had nothing to do, just wait for the next four boxes to accumulate. I hated Position One most because if you missed a beat and got behind the three metal tubes would descend and spray you with syrup, concentrate, or vinegar instead of filling the bottles like they're supposed to. We would get a break for lunch and sometimes, unexpectedly, when part of the machine broke down.

ORANGES UNDERCOVER

Orange juice and lemon juice have been used for centuries as invisible ink. And though you would think that for the coherence of this story, the men in the underground movement would have communicated using secret writing from the juice of oranges, oranges were not the only undercover fruit. The truth is they used bananas—they would cut slits in the peels and slip into them coded notes covered in a thin film of rubber. Could the Engineer have used a banana instead of an orange? A banana peel is harder to hold together, harder to prevent from browning rapidly and revealing the explosives inside. Besides, a *banana between the hearts* sounds even more ridiculous than an orange.

THE WATCHMAKER, SEGMENT IV

In the Watchmaker's theater the audience sees a small mechanical human. The audience asks: *Who is the king?* and the automaton writes the answer silently with its metal quill. *Who gave you life?* and it reproduces an exact copy of the Watchmaker's signature. To the audience's delight the mechanical figure draws landscapes, buildings, a portrait of Eros. *The Writer,* as it was called, conjures whatever the audience desires. One dreams that under the right circumstances *The Writer* could put a quill to paper and produce the intricate secrets that made the orange tree possible.

A FAILURE OF ORANGE

In first grade I imagined myself a magician and took on the mission of astounding others with tricks. But the acts were always too difficult to follow through on without the necessary discipline and so the plastic wand, the cups, and the coins remained unmastered. Whatever illusions I was able to successfully perform I couldn't help but immediately reveal to the audience of grandparents and younger children.

COUNTING IN ORANGE IN POMEGRANATE

The average number of segments in an orange is said to be ten. The average number of pomegranate seeds in Jewish tradition is said to be 613, the same as the number of *mitzvot,* or good deeds. The pomegranate is one of the seven species of the Land of Israel, and considered to be a holy fruit. To me the orange is a *daily* fruit, the segments adding up to an ordinary number. This doesn't mean that in the moment of pulling apart segment from segment my fingers, lips, and tongue don't feel a current of anticipation. When it comes to breaking apart pomegranates I know of three kinds of people: those who tap the fruit gently with the back of a spoon, those who carefully undo seed from rind submerged in a bowl full of water, and those who pick up the pomegranate and in one motion smash it on the ground to eat from the opened fragments.

The Engineer's greatest concern was that the oranges would dry out and reveal the splinters that held them together. He was worried about the seams showing, the illusion collapsing, the unwitting audience of guards seeing through the trick. The Engineer made three oranges: two for the two men—packed with shrapnel and explosives—and a hollow one for himself, a test orange. The two oranges were sent to the men, carried in the metal dessert bowl, and the third the Engineer kept on the mantel in his cell where he could study the fruit, watch it progress in time. From that particular angle the orange could be seen by the British guard pacing outside. On the first day the orange looked whole. On the second day the orange looked whole. But on the morning of the third day the thick Shamouti peel finally started to give way, and the seams began to show. The Engineer sent word there was no more time. The order was given, the two men detonated that night.

A FAILURE OF ORANGE

In first grade I imagined myself an engineer and decided to construct a car. I convinced my grandfather to help me, by which I mean I gave him directions and he tried as best he could to make them work. We took apart a discarded baby carriage from one of the kibbutz baby homes, kept the base and wheels and placed a wood crate we constructed on top of them. The "car" did not go very far. My grandmother dubbed us *lo-yutzlakhim*, "men of frequent failures," in Yiddish-accented Hebrew, and for years would bring up the image of the two of us standing in front of the cart with tools in our hands, uncertain what to do.

A SUBSTITUTE ORANGE

What if instead of grenades soldiers carried around pomegranates, two pomegranates hanging from their vests, ready to burst—red against their olive uniforms, the cracks so wide that the many rubied seeds were already showing, an unstoppable shiny, sticky sweetness. What if in war films the hero called out "Pomegranate!" instead of "Grenade!" and then dove on top of the fruit to protect his friends (always a "he" in war films). No noble sacrifices then, only a crushed red under his chest.

A SUBSTITUTE ORANGE

After the explosion the scene in the jail cell must have been terrible to see. It would have been red there. It would have reached everywhere. The two men needed an orange accelerated to human time, a fruit that lasted a single beat, that would undo them quickly—the Engineer made a very short fuse, only one second long, in case one of the guards noticed. What if instead the two men slowed themselves down to botanical time, stood entirely still, allowed the seeds to take hold in their chests, to form roots, embracing each other so long the orange tree could grow between them, and then instead of red we would have seen *Citrons, oranges and greens / Flowering over the skin.* In the story we know the two men did detonate the orange between their chests. I think of that bound machine—a heart | an orange filled with shrapnel | a heart—and how for one second it all beat together.

A SUBSTITUTE ORANGE

"Rimon between the hearts"—and though *rimon* means a grenade, if we imagine it to be a pomegranate, it is a third heart between the two men.

THE INVENTOR, SEGMENT V

The Inventor never saw his invention realized. Only after his death was one part of the patented prototype purchased by a company for further development. He never saw the arresting hum of a wide orchard intelligently watered by a central mind, each tree, each branch, each fruit an extension of a watering machine.

THE OBJECT IN ORANGE

In archival footage we see men and women sitting on the floor of a dusty factory individually wrapping the oranges for shipping overseas. It is easy to forget that the fruit was not only held as a treasured object, but peeled, split, and eaten. It's easy to forget that the oranges became part of our body.

THE ORANGE IN THE BEGINNING

In the beginning the fruit is a unitary sphere. As soon as our fingernail makes its first impression in the peel, there are many ways the fruit can unravel. The main tension in an orange is between the peel and the center. Perhaps you have seen this tension: there is enough electric current in an orange to power a light bulb.

UNDER THE PEEL OF AN ORANGE

The thing about the orange is you never know if it's the orange you've been craving until you uncover it. Like when eating fruit from a bowl: if you eat a delicious pomegranate seed you want to eat another to recapture the sweetness in your mouth, and if you eat a bland seed you want to eat another in hopes of repairing the flavor.

THE WATCHMAKER, SEGMENT V

In his home the Watchmaker shaped time. If he woke up early, all of the clocks moved ahead and the household rose from their beds. If he was running behind, all of the clocks moved back and the Watchmaker was never late. In his hands time was malleable and conformed around him as the center. And on the stage the Watchmaker turned the oranges into objects of desire—it was not their sweetness that made it so, but the Watchmaker's ability to replace their organic unfolding with the determined ticks of an automaton, accelerating their slow story.

THE ORANGE AT THE END OF LANGUAGE

The orange reveals a desire for an end to language. The audience is dumbstruck with wonder then fills their mouths with fruit. Two men refuse to testify at their own trial then shred their bodies. The well-irrigated orange grows at a pace we cannot hear. Oranges, however, only fill us temporarily. Every act of speechlessness carries within it the seed of talk: "Did you see . . ." "Have you heard . . ." "Taste this orange . . ."

THE ORANGE IN THE CENTER

Do you see the orange tree? In an orchard the trees are never in isolation. That is, one cannot see a tree by itself—its wholeness is only as part of the orchard. And of course, no one can *see* the orange tree. One knows that the foliage of one tree ends and another's begins, but it is difficult to tell where—from far away or up close.

AN ORANGE'S REFUSAL

Oranges are a sticky fruit. I hate the sensation that clings to my fingers. If I eat an orange, if I peel it, if I divide its segments, I want to know there is a faucet nearby—even an irrigation spigot will do, or at the very least a water bottle—just to make sure that the skin has an exit strategy.

THIS ORANGE THAT IS NOT AN ANIMAL

We can imagine ourselves as birds or beasts, but the orange tree is impenetrable. We can raise our arms and hold them out as limbs, our fingers as the smallest branches, our hair as foliage—but how long will it take until we grow bored and restless? Try to imagine the slowness of water moving through your veins as xylem or sugar moving through your arteries as phloem and the slow creep of the fluid, which seems to go nowhere at all, will make you want to shake every part of your body just to know that you're alive. The orange tree is impenetrable, so we turn it into a marvel.

To make the orange grenades the Engineer would collect slivers of metal shrapnel from the prison machine shop, he would hide these in the books he borrowed from the prison library. He would work on the grenades in the small window of time between the arrival and departure of the guards. When he heard them coming back he and his cellmate would pretend to be playing backgammon.

BORING ORANGE

The articles and exhibits depicting the story of the two men are tacky and off-putting. They feel like hand-drawn posters made by education officers in the military: some clichéd lines about bravery written with felt markers on paperboard. In the Museum of Underground Prisoners there is an installation showing two life-size mannequins in a jail cell, embracing each other with an orange between them. Something about the way they stand there, frozen mid-embrace, seems to say that the only people who still come to watch them are coerced fifth graders on a class trip.

THE ORANGE AND THE POMEGRANATE, CONTAINMENT

The sharp pointed star of an orange blossom grows into a near-perfect sphere. If one studies the growth of a pomegranate, one notices that after the outgrowing petals explode, the forward motion reverses, the plant appears to retract, and the fruit becomes a ball, with many chambers—nothing like what you thought. If one watches the tree for many years, a pomegranate runs in a loop of explosion containment explosion.

THE ORANGE IN GEOMETRY

If it feels like oranges are everywhere that is because they are everywhere. Once you trace their movement you begin to see their sticky residue all over. Objects of desire that they are, humans carry them wherever the seeds grow—wherever their roots will take. Or else—objects of human desire that they are, humans carry them wherever sweetness is wanted. Which is everywhere.

A FAILURE OF ORANGE

I did not last long in the factory. A shift once a week or so starting in middle school and half the number of days of every school vacation. In high school I picked up extra shifts over the summers—if I covered enough of these the kibbutz would fund my participation in the senior class trip to Greece. Instead I took the money and went on a trip with my girlfriend to Paris, then London. My last stretch of working the line was in the nine months between the end of twelfth grade and my draft date. In kibbutz terms that is not very long. My grandfather lasted in the factory until he turned eighty-five—he started falling from the gangplanks surrounding his machine because of inner ear trouble and had to retire. I don't know how he handled a lifetime of repetitive action. How he found the discipline. How he could participate in the dull industrial project of this collective community without complaining, this community of members who could do what I could not.

THE ORANGE AS DESIRE

The men who embraced the orange embraced it for its ability to annihilate. Desire turns to death. Were they not caught carrying grenades outside the prison they wouldn't have been inside the prison. The Inventor only wants to know when the trees are thirsty and when they're not. His device embraces the tree, grasps its leaf between metallic pincers to measure just how wide, how swollen with water it is. The Watchmaker was only able to entice his audiences by speeding up botanical time—his automaton was, in a way, the first time-lapse video. We now quickly click from one film of accelerated time to the next, and for every sequence of a dandelion opening up in a meadow there is also a whale carcass disintegrating at the bottom of the ocean.

THE ENGINEER, SEGMENT VII

His eyes sparkle whenever he speaks of mechanical solutions to a problem or of events that unfold like the silk leaves of an automated tree. To turn the oranges into objects of desire he introduced them into a machine. They were hollowed out and filled with shrapnel and explosives. We can assume that the Engineer consumed the pulp, created the space for the explosives by taking that part of the orange into his mouth. But the Engineer never speaks of it.

FAR FROM ORANGES

When I worked in the juice factory I knew the oranges were there even though I never touched them. Walking across the kibbutz before the start of a shift I could see the discarded peels in piles outside the factory fence. I could see the new fruit floating down the troughs on a mechanical river as they were being washed. But on the factory floor where I worked, oranges only arrived in their distilled form—a concentrated syrup shooting out of three metal pipes, filling three bottles at a time. The color appeared nothing like the fruit, nothing like the orange that came from the orchards.

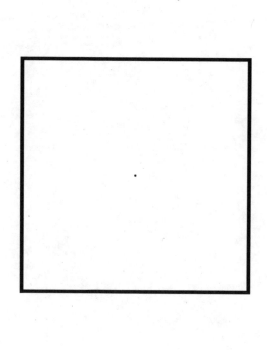

The nautilus's eye is a pinhole. The human eye depends on a lens. When we reach out to hold a shell do we stop to consider that between us and the solidity of the shell are many layers—iris and lens, skin and nerve? The nautilus's eye contracts and expands to let in the light it needs and, in the process, seawater. Light and salt flow in and out of the pinhole as the nautilus senses. To perceive only through sight is to exclude the material of the world. In the act of sensing, the shell remains apart from us.

WOULDN'T IT

My four-year-old hand stretches into the space between my parents' bed and the cold floor tiles, the contours of their bodies are still. My fingers want to close around the metal of the rifle. Every night I wake up in the middle of the night, bend my body down, and look upside down under the bed to search for the silhouette.

My cousin, on leave from his base, is cleaning his gun. I ask him what that stink is. And he says, "That is the sweet smell of gunpowder, you either love it or you hate it."

My mind swings wildly between caring obsessively about the cleanliness of my boots and rifle and not caring at all. In the height of mania I need to see my face reflected in my boot-tips, there can't be a single grain of sand inside the barrel of my M-16.

It would be lovely and terrible to live in a world made of glass. Everything would be so fragile and transparent. We would refract all light and constantly make rainbows. And breaking one of us would mean, perhaps, breaking all of us.

In the Israeli Defense Forces' easiest basic training, the military's future drivers, cooks, quartermasters, pencil pushers, mechanics, and yes, intelligence analysts line up for their first firing range. They ask the corporal in charge what will happen if they get a bull's-eye with every shot; will they be reassigned as elite snipers? The corporal orders the asthmatics, the flatfooted, the rejects, the confused, the bullies, and the nerds to shut up and give him twenty.

The first gun I ever own is a blue plastic water gun. I hold it upside down and pretend I'm ironing clothes.

It would be lovely and terrible to live in a world made of leaves. Everything would be so soft and crunchy. If any of us hurt we would all rush to cover. If any of us felt uncomfortable we could simply sink into one another. We would be green until it was time to be red. We would be red until it was time to be brown. We would be brown until it was time to be dead. We would be dead until it was time to be green.

My grandfather's Mauser is here somewhere. All of the grandchildren are looking for it. Where are the hidden cavities in his house? Behind a trapdoor in the shower ceiling is an old landline. A cable connected it to the underground explosives lab. I crawl through the hidden passage in his bedroom closet and into the bathroom. The grandchildren are searching for the gun. There are hollow spaces between the living room cabinets and the walls.

The butt of an M-16 is hollow and contains a sort of secret compartment, and because we received these guns as aid from the US government, and because they're so old, I make the joke that hidden inside are the finger bones of Viet Cong soldiers. Not many people find this funny.

If I release the trigger right after I shoot, the rifle jams. If I take a breath, I can keep firing.

It would be lovely and terrible to live in a world made of Lego. We would all fit together consistently. Every foot would have a perfect round anchor, and our faces would carry a permanent sickle smile.

A soldier in my unit tells me how sexy it feels to fire a Glock at the firing range she takes her father to. In the next breath she tells me how difficult it is to decide between asking him to buy her a new Volkswagen Beetle or a Peugeot 206.

The soldier's frame fills the entirety of the bus seat, his head leans against the window. My long hair covers my adolescent face and my knee hurts at the spot where it's pressed by the barrel of his rifle.

The 1996 Lonely Planet guide to Israel describes tourists being shocked when they see soldiers in civilian dress dancing in nightclubs with their M-16s. The guide asks the reader to understand that the punishment for misplacing one's gun in the Israel Defense Forces is severe, and many soldiers choose to take the rifle with them rather than risk losing it.

It would be lovely and terrible to live in a world made of gold. We would wonder if we were the outside wrappers of expensive chocolates. Our pillows would be bullions and we'd be off the hook for greed.

I beg my dad to fire just one bullet. We're walking down the road at night, no one else is around, and he is the guard on duty. My head reaches his hip, and my steps try to keep in rhythm with his. He tells me that it's too dangerous, that the bullet could hit someone. I tell him to shoot into the road, that way it won't hit anyone. He tells me it's late and that the sound would wake up the entire kibbutz. I tell him to fire just one bullet, that's all.

A friend who has never served tells me guns are not good or evil, people are good or evil. I tell him guns were made by people.

During the first night of officer training I look around and understand I'm not the same as everyone else. I lack ambition, I lack drive, I lack purpose. All the other future officers are intently cleaning their M-16s, the parts spread before them on stretches of flannel fabric. My body makes a decision and I fall ill. In the morning I drop out and return to my base.

It would be lovely and terrible to live in a world made of stone. A single break would take millions of years of convection to undo. Perhaps then we would be more cautious with our actions.

My father claims to have been able to strip, clean, and assemble an Uzi faster than anyone in his base, but he's never used one in combat.

I'm heading back to the bus stop from the military recruitment base, where a doctors' committee has ruled me fit to serve in a noncombat capacity as soon as I turn eighteen. A soldier sees me walking toward the stop and calls out: "*Akhi* [my brother], what's the time?" I tell him, and think to myself that the era in which I am a brother to other men has begun.

It would be lovely and terrible to live in a world made of steam. How could we tell ourselves apart? Flesh and blood visitors would enjoy having their pores opened and their sinuses cleared.

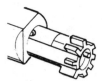

The barrel of the rifle is pointing toward the sky; I'm holding the charging handle back tight. If I let go the bolt will spring into place, crushing the digits of the officer who is fingering the insides of my M-16, searching for forgotten bullets.

It would be lovely and terrible to live in a world made of milk. Our skin would be so soft before we turn sour.

Guard duty, and the rifle that comes with it, is every five weeks. Close enough so I don't forget how to use it. Far enough apart so that I don't get used to it.

It would be lovely and terrible to live in a world made of margins. Over there, the line. Over there, beyond the line.

The lights of the West Bank settlement make the whole dark world look orange. I occasionally glance at the ██████████████ I'm guarding, but mostly I sink into my padded winter suit and read my book. A settler-boy shows up and I pay him no mind, just tell him to stay away from the ██████████. He comes up to me and, gyrating his hips, simulates fucking the barrel of my M-16 with his twelve-year-old crotch.

It would be lovely and terrible to live in a world made of wheels. To be together would be. To be together would be. To be together would be precarious.

They try to steal your arms—your rifle that is—when you're asleep. So sleep with your gun under you. Grasp the strap in your hooked fingers.

It would be lovely and terrible to live in a world made of cork. Enjoy it once, on special occasions.

It would be lovely and terrible to live in a world made of yarn. Beware the space cat.

It would be lovely and terrible to live in a world made of matches. Intimacy would be cautious; the risks would be known.

He tells me it's a hostile village down there. They all know it's just a matter of time before someone from over there will try to infiltrate the base, which is why we're on patrol. He tells me we should sit down and take a break, hide in the toolshed from the officers for a little while. Shouldn't we keep patrolling, I ask him, I thought he said it was a hostile village down there; isn't it a matter of time before something happens? That's right, he says, it's just a matter of time.

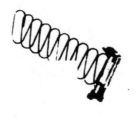

A two-week assignment on this base means taking the 02:00 to 08:00 shift every night, and watching the so-called hostile village as it wakes for another day of Ramadan. Sleepers are woken early by the sound of banging tins and fireworks so as to take their predawn meal. The fireworks sound like gunshots, and I wonder, Should I call it in, or should I not?

It would be lovely and terrible to live in a world made of clay. Dirt our eyes; dirt our ears; dirt our mouth.

The image is the first of the dead I see coming into form in the red light of the darkroom—a shot taken in the Yom Kippur war from the vantage point of a tank turret, printed in the spring of senior year twenty-five years later. This is not my photo, though I am the one looking. This is not my lover's photo, though she borrowed the negative from her father. This is not her father's photo, though he was the one who released the shutter. Can we say instead the image belongs to the dead? I begin to see one leg, one arm, tangled robes, and Sinai sand stretching in every direction. Right before I take the photo out of the developer, footprints anf tank treads appear and divide the desert.

PASSPORT

In the high school darkroom I see his features start to form, but I dislike the borders, where I want him to show, and he appears out of the paper—cloudlike. Some drops undoing them now.

I sit and watch over his body. When my mother opened the door of my childhood the bed, too old for the room. I walk to Neve Noam, the old-age home my grandmother such slowness before. He and I exist in our own stream of time. My sister walks in and *bridge / is a narrow bridge / is a narrow bridge. / The whole wide world is a narrow be afraid at all. And most of all / and most of all / do not be afraid at all.*

On Ilford photographic paper his skin looks like metal. The flame from one candle turns the dark. My focus is sharp and his chest hair burns white. It would take a magnifying his eyes closed he jokes that in his village in Czechoslovakia this is how they would

My grandfather came to Palestine at twenty-two, the same age I was when I left Israel. the day he drove a truck for the kibbutz cooperative and at night he was the liaison the communal laundromat. When the British raided the kibbutz for weapons as part ammo out of my grandfather's room under their skirts. My grandfather had a secret

On leave, I drop off my three sets of uniform at the laundromat and walk to my them about the War of 1948, though I have no recollection of why I do so, perhaps adjacent to our kibbutz. Some here say they were seasonal mud abodes for farmers Perhaps they call them "temporary shelters" to feel better, but they had names: Zelephi tell me that they don't know. The villagers left. When I ask again they say they were

At the end of his life, while still able to speak, my grandfather would tell me he had requires complete conviction at every juncture. The ability to write each point into behind, of choosing to go to the kibbutz.

the edges too stark. So I take a paintbrush, dip it into the developer and paint only

stray and reveal the lines of his throat. Lines I was trying to avoid, but there is no

bedroom to let me know about the phone call I was not surprised. I felt too large for

jokes was named after me. And then I sit and watch over his body. I have not known

suggests we sing him a song. We pick a Hasidic tune: *The whole wide world is a narrow*

bridge / is / a / narrow / bridge. And most of all / most of all / do not be afraid / do not

my grandfather's body into a topography—one half the light side of the hill, the other

glass to tell where the tips of the follicles blur. When I ask him to pose lying down with

position the dead for one last portrait.

He was recruited to the Haganah, one of the Jewish underground movements. During

to a team of chemists who were manufacturing explosives in a hidden room beneath

of what we call "The Black Sabbath," it's said women smuggled guns, grenades, and

compartment, what we call a "slick," under his cot.

grandparents' house to thank them for the care package they sent. I end up asking

because of a report I was translating that week. I heard there were Palestinian villages

from the West Bank hills who came down to tend their fields during the rainy season.

and Menshiya. When I ask my grandparents what happened to these villagers they

"made to leave."

no regrets. None. Over and over he would say this. To live a life with such certainty

one single line—the point of leaving Czechoslovakia, the point of leaving his family

In other accounts the explosives are manufactured in a hidden room beneath the

Made to leave can mean many things, depending on who is telling the story. A website
villages on its interactive map. What matters to me is that people were in a place,

I watch his body all morning until one of the Neve Noam nurses comes in to tell me
my cousin. She has not seen him yet, she still has not said goodbye. She walks to his
me and I ask Do I need to go in to see to him? and she says No, no one needs to see
is brought to the cemetery in a plain plywood box. And then he is carried by me and

If you were to look for remains of Zelephi and Menshiya you would find no walls or
borders to separate one plot from the next. They are low and thorny, full of prickly
grandparents' generation planted tall rows of cypress trees to divide the citrus

In other accounts the villages emptied out before the real war even started, in

In the airplane bathroom I make the switch. At the midpoint between the two
jeans, which are dangling around my ankles, and put it in my money sock. I take out
The tip of the belt almost touches the floor of the airplane bathroom where there's

These actions are reversed if I am moving against the rotation of the earth.

Neither document can reconcile a feeling (of this is not my place). Though both

We walk under the elms in Providence. In the classroom I'm her Hebrew TA and
oldest one, University Hall, was built by slave labor, though without the proper
builder's accounting ledgers and now we know whose hands built those walls. The
from Kibbutz Givat Haim Ichud and she is from Ramallah. But out here, under the
summer plans. The pink of buds is everywhere. She explains to me the route she has
to experience. I ask her if it's difficult. And in English she says, "It's very difficult."

Across their visa pages passports never capture lines. Only points of entry and exit.

bottom of a well, not the communal laundromat.

dedicated to documenting the mass exile of Palestinians in 1948 does not show the two and they are there no longer.

they are ready to move him now, so I leave the room and walk to the lobby where I see room where they are moving his body, but immediately turns around, walks toward *this moment.* Somehow there is a gap. I lose track of his body. The next moment he five other grandchildren, just like he always said he wanted.

doors or windows. The only markers are tangles of cacti, which the villagers used as pear fruit in the summer that, despite its sweetness, is too much labor to eat. My orchards—a dusty green wall made of fine-pointed teeth breaking the horizon.

December 1947.

countries I take out the blue passport with the eagle on it from the left pocket of my the blue passport with the menorah on it and put it in the left pocket of my jeans. a drop of urine left by someone else.

documents can evoke a feeling (of this is my place).

she's my student. Around us are dignified brick buildings. Later I find out that the documentation no one was aware of that history. Scholars recently found the weathervane on top of the building points east, toward us. Across the Atlantic I am elms, we're both members of the class of '09 and we're talking in English about our to take to get back home, the many checks and roadblocks, none of which I've had And I have nothing left to say, so I don't.

For a long time whenever I sat on the toilet and smelled my own shit I thought of whether I wanted it or not.

VISAS אשרות

In the weeks following air travel I wake up in the middle of the night not knowing who between me and my face is far. All I know is out of reach.

They say the dead have the best view in the kibbutz: lush citrus orchards spreading canopy of pines—discarded needles everywhere.

In hindsight we think we know what these movements across space and time mean with larger ones. But to us now, what do our points and lines mean at all? We hear key *Middle East—War—Refugees—Palestine—Israel*. We make: *a story*. Points turning into story. A document reduces a complicated reality to a flatness, which does not mean

When I first left the country my parents continued to receive notices requiring me to the exit stamps from my passport to use as evidence.

When I cross the border, the border police database is supposed to connect to the actively choose to desert, but neither do I stay long enough in Israel for the military

Headstones capture little more than points of entry and exit. Up until the kibbutz a visitor can walk the perimeter road, turn right by the communal pool, walk through hold a sense of urgency in asserting an individual life rather than one-of-many: a

There is the moment when the officer at the airport swipes my passport and I look sweaty fingerprints my hands have made and I wipe them with the edge of my

Though meant to be an occasion of public record, the stamping of a passport is a

There is the official gesture that occurs right before a stamp hits—the official's hand metal and rubber, forcing the adjustable dates to turn, inking the name of the airport

my grandfather. This was not a connection in my mind that I liked, but it happened,

I am. My face hovers two inches above me. The borders are too sharp. The distance

toward the West Bank, the punctuating rows of cypress trees, the graves under a tall

in relation to the larger forces of history. Backward, we see how our small story fits

words and turn them into a narrative. Say *Palestine 1948* and we fill in blanks: *Europe*—

timelines then timelines into feelings. I can't tell stories because the passport is not *a*

that the reality is this. But neither is it not.

report to reserve military duty. They had to prove that I wasn't there. I would fax them

reserve soldier database, instantly telling them whether I'm AWOL or not. I don't

notices to find me there.

privatized, the only information available on the stones was a name and two dates. Now

the double row of cypresses and view the gravestones made after privatization. These

biblical verse, "beloved grandmother," an icon of a paintbrush or an airplane.

down at the marble surface below the Plexiglas window of her booth and I see the

sleeve. I always wait for her to give me a second glance.

private moment.

pressing down on the handle, the mechanism causing downward motion to rotate

surrounded by a border onto paper—a pressure, an authentication of a passage.

In recent years Israeli authorities have pushed more and more citizens to link their
resist this bureaucracy. A long row of shiny automated kiosks greets travelers as they
their palm print, allow another photo to be taken. Greeters call out: "Israeli passport
are more and more automated kiosks and fewer and fewer manned booths. As a result,
and longer, as they watch those who surrender pass them by.

I renewed my Israeli passport in 2002, which is also the year I left.

I renewed my Israeli passport again in 2012, though when asked how long I've lived

Do not be fooled by the stamps inside my expired US passport: the snake-green of
to you of *what* happened—only the *when* of the beginning and the end.

In the spring of 2002 the authorities changed the law for dual citizens. From that
passports when exiting or entering Israel.

My word processing software wants to correct *all bearers* to *pall bearers*.

My Israeli passport is a self-contained object. It only shows Ben Gurion Airport's round
out, but it doesn't say where to or from.

In my passport there are two exceptions to the uniformity of Israeli stamps. The first

If I were to say that when I arrived at the bed and breakfast in Amsterdam and I
father, my grandmother's brother, took over the family inheritance and she never
when later I realized on those cobbled streets that in August in Amsterdam it is only
I saw, an overpriced Eurotrashy sweatshirt, which I then lost in a different country,
hours, thinking, *This is the most profound shit I've ever read in my life*, which most
through the streets back to the bed and breakfast realizing that it was located right
in their windows, and the johns walking up and down the street, one in particular
not be an exotification of the truth.

passports to biometric data. Though legally still a voluntary option, it is difficult to
disembark from their flight, promising them a faster process if only they'll surrender
holders, this way!" pointing to the machines, tricking the uninformed. Every year there
every year the lines of those who refuse to impart their palms or faces become longer

outside the country I answer with the phrase *on and off* and round down the years.

Mexico, the two tones of Switzerland, the flat black of Cyprus. They will say nothing

moment on, all bearers of Israeli passports were required to use only their Israeli

exit stamps and the square entry stamps. It only shows when I come in and when I get

shows a three-day stay in Holland. The second shows an entry and exit in Prague.

ran into my second cousin there, the one whom I hadn't seen in years ever since his
spoke to him again, and my cousin recognized me, but I didn't recognize him, and
T-shirt weather if you don't stand in the shade and I had to buy the first warm thing
and that later in a coffee shop I read the same page of my book over and over for two
likely had to do with the "organic" marijuana I smoked there earlier, then walking
in the heart of the Red Light District, and seeing the half-naked prostitutes standing
going back and forth, trying to decide whether to go in or not—when I say this it will

When Israelis speak to one another they refer to Israel as *The Land* and no other
been eighteen months since I've left The Land.

I'm looking for contrasting light to bring this story to life, but passports and airports

And if I wanted a different light where would I look for it? I mean light from essential

If I were to say that when I first arrived I wanted to leave the airport to explore this
and they were killed, the city which he left to go to Palestine when he was about the
about to catch a transit flight to go to the Mediterranean coast of Spain with my lover
farms for the following three months, but instead it was pouring rain for three weeks
us stay in a leaky, moldy trailer, where we got bedbugs, and where our first job was to
the farm one day when the farmer wasn't around, hitchhiking to the next town, where
them eat his olive trees to death because he loved them so much, where we couldn't
sheets using the laundry machine's highest temperature setting, but we couldn't bring
the next town we found a farm on a cliff overlooking the sea, where the people were
a fundamentalist Christian cult, which thought Israel would one day kill all the Arabs,
of dolphins leaping through the waves as we were walking on the beach below majestic
arrived in Prague on our way out of Europe I again wanted to explore the city, but it
to buy Pilsner beer, and also a gift of salami for my grandfather, which I hoped tasted

Whenever I returned to Israel my grandfather would always say: "So, Noam, what I
offer no answer.

When I left The Land it was not a declaration. For whatever reason I keep moving
itinerants, refugees, and immigrants. I simply can't think more than a day or two into
see the passage of time except in hindsight.

On the other hand, when I do leave, I feel the round stamp yearning to be

There are days when I leaf through my passport, trying to recall my narrative lines
takes over and a reconstruction of the lines becomes more and more difficult.

qualifiers are necessary. As in, *I always fly Lufthansa when I return to The Land,* or *It's*

are by their nature flat and gray.

colors, not from ones superimposed on gray to make it seem other than it is.

city where my grandfather once lived, where his family lived, before the war came
same age I was when I left Israel, but that I was just passing through, that I was just
where we were supposed to be enjoying the always-sunny weather working on organic
straight, and that in our first farm we lived with a misanthropic anarchist, who had
build a teepee around the hole in the ground that was to be our toilet, and that we left
we met another farmer, an expat German ex-priest who raised sheep and was letting
get rid of the bedbugs so we escaped to the next town, right after we washed all his
ourselves to tell him we might have infected his house, and that when we reached
friendly, and we thought we finally found a place to rest, but then discovered that it was
and where we discovered that the bedbugs were still following us, and where the sight
cliffs failed to make us happy, so we decided to go back to Israel, and that when we
was January and far too cold, so we had to stay in the airport, and use our last euros
like a memory of home—when I say this it will also not be an exotification of the truth.

really want to know is—are you here or are you there?" And I would smile weakly and

forward. Someone suggested I shouldn't be surprised—I come from generations of
the future, that if leaving or returning is an indecision it persists due to my inability to

bookended by the square stamp. I also resent this feeling.

through the points of the stamps. After a while the repetition of the same ink forms

A week or so after I collected another square stamp, my mother called to tell me that our kibbutz has no street names and the driver wouldn't know where to go. I climbed didn't know but that my grandfather was almost ninety-six, so something like this can I don't know why I said this, except for maybe the need to appease authority figures.

When I walked into my grandparents' house, the paramedic behind me, I saw my remind me of a time that was sadder, I would hear him gasping for air and the sound of would never leave. That all hard moments would move toward the sharpness of that touch and leave. It is no longer the destination that all sad thoughts move toward.

At first, after he was released from the hospital, we tried to take care of my grandfather none of us could lift him.

I am trying to understand where I pass through. There are gates I can look toward, and the neon lights of the departure hall wash out the remaining details.

Clicking on profile after profile of matches on OkCupid I keep encountering the that moment I move over this possible future lover who is saying: *I am a traveler, an* the paper, the ways in which we allow bureaucracy to permeate our desire.

When I stop by for a visit, my grandmother and her caregiver are standing over him. He his legs up for them, and it is the smoothest skin I've ever touched. My grandmother to remove so it doesn't get soiled. Because my grandmother has no short-term memory correcting and exposing. My grandfather doesn't say anything the whole time, but

He died two days after my thirtieth birthday and one day before I was supposed inconvenience anyone.

A month after I got my last round stamp my father sent me a photograph of the the uniform concrete blocks.

my grandfather wasn't well and asked if I could meet the ambulance at the gate because

onto the ambulance and the paramedic asked me what was wrong and I told him that I

happen—*you know?*—turning toward him as if he was the one in need of reassurance.

grandfather convulsing on his bed. For a long time after, whenever I felt sad, and as if to

the tongue in his throat—*clomp clomp clomp*. For a long time after I thought that sound

memory. Now it surprises me when the memory does arrive—its edges a sadness I can

Over time the grief weakens and that destination becomes one of many points.

in his house. He couldn't move anymore. He was so small and fragile and weak but

thinking that one day I will understand. But the future is unclear, the past is murky,

same answer for the question *Six things I could never do without*: "My passport." In

explorer, sophisticated and adventurous. All I hear is the sound of the stamp hitting

is defecating in the bed, but they are too weak to change his diaper by themselves. I hold

worries he is too exposed and so covers his lower body with a blanket, which I then have

we repeat these back and forth gestures over and over—her noticing and covering, me

whenever I look into his eyes he again recognizes me and smiles.

to leave the country, and everyone said he was always like this, never wanting to

gravestone. It stands out from the surrounding graves—a slab of natural stone among

A week after they put in the stone my grandmother visited his grave. She saw two men than everyone else's.

During a short visit home a friend from the US comes to see me at my kibbutz. We walk dining hall, kindergarten, elementary school, children's farm, pool. I want to show her passage. She points out to me that *There didn't use to be a fence here* is the statement

Right around when I left the country for the first time, the kibbutz underwent a process meant that public spaces were now divided and access had to be restricted.

There is one barrier present in the kibbutz that was there before and is still there one spot in the cemetery though, below the military graves, on the hill descending to the poles. A calculated step over the barbs and you're out of the perimeter.

When the British controlled Palestine my grandfather transported undocumented he himself had a signed affidavit from the British authorities that allowed him legal

One night the operation failed. A member of the Jewish underground was actually same night they arrived. After picking them up from the beach, my grandfather turned was sent to the Latrun prison camp. The refugees were sent to prison camps on the

Nothing stands of the British prison camp in Latrun. Arab and Jewish forces my grandfather was imprisoned, there now resides a park called Mini Israel. Three One of the models is of the kibbutz juice factory where I worked as a teenager, where inside to see the assembly line. A human figure the length of their index finger

In other accounts my grandfather is arrested and sent to Latrun after being caught

These places of passage contain us. There are points that determine whether our bodies, that our minds can move past these barriers. But the truth is that our minds

from the kibbutz sanding down the gravestone, making sure it wouldn't stand taller

paths I have walked many times. We stop by the community's defining institutions: these formative places. Everywhere I go there is a boundary where I remember an open I most often make.

of privatization. This meant that what was once shared was now privately owned. This

now—a surrounding fence. Raids and infiltrations were always a possibility. There is the orchards where time has trampled a section of the wire. Vines have taken down

refugees into the interior under the cover of night. But he was always proud that entry into the country.

a British spy and blew their cover. Those undocumented refugees were captured the the truck to head to the interior but British soldiers were already waiting for him. He island of Cyprus.

demolished most of the structures during intense fighting in the 1948 war. Near where hundred and eighty-five small-scale models of different Israeli landmarks stand there. my grandfather worked until the age of eighty-five. Children stand around and peer stands encased in glass, watching oranges the size of ladybugs pass by.

for hiding weapons, not refugees.

physical bodies can move forward. We can say that these points only contain our can only wander so far, before we realize that they too are restrained.

I do not sleep well on airplanes. On a long journey, one where even a little sleep helps, specific haze when I disembark—after the plane lands and I wake and all the lights I realize then that my passport is gone, it is not in the left pocket of my jeans, and in this country. There is the fever of the blood rising to the surface when the body and smallness. I spot two tall men in uniform, and though they are not looking at passport, pages turned to my photograph, comparing. *I must have dropped it*, I say, came from.

After collecting my suitcase and before passing through customs, I can't wait any longer baggage claim area. The room is a maze in itself and when I exit through the door looking expectantly, waiting for arrivals to come through the main gate. If I move ungoverned space. And I find myself confused at how this hole is even possible. So

When I was younger I thought of my passport romantically. Like a spy I had two, I required to carry both, carrying both always feels a little like breaking the law. In the

Before they tore it down to build the larger and more spacious Neve Noam to house the infirmary. It was called the *ee'zoo'la'tor*, from the German for "isolator," meaning were any old to house there, they housed the infirm. Before there were any infirm they because there were no elderly. All of the founders were young.

We can track the ways in which the creation of borders echo beyond the present: a walk through the gate or not, the line we can cross or not, the documents we have as of an inside and an outside—outside the present moment.

Rarely do people notice I am not a native English speaker. When I do slip and am usually around different shades of the sound "ee." In Hebrew there is only one, like between *i* and *ea* and so say "live" when I want to say "leave," and "leave" when I

The existence of a document means there's a reality that made it possible. It doesn't

my parents send me away with one of their sleeping pills, called Stilnox. There is a

are blinding. I wander around and around the luggage belt searching for my suitcase.

though I have the other one hidden in the money sock, it is not the right one to use

is caught out of place in a structure it cannot control. Embarrassment, confusion,

me, I can tell they are looking for me. I move toward them and they are holding my

and they return the document to me silently and move back to whatever point they

to pee, and enter the men's restroom in the Newark Liberty International Airport's

I thought I entered I find myself on the other side. There, people are holding signs,

forward I will bypass the customs line and immigration line and simply slip into this

instead I turn around with my luggage, find the first door, and join the line.

could choose whom to be: Israeli or American. And even though I am bureaucratically

end though, these are not forged documents, only two related to the same self.

the newly aged, the kibbutz housed the very old in a long narrow building next to

separating the infected individual body from the healthy collective body. Before there

housed the stricken. At the kibbutz's beginning, death from old age was not possible

whole series of struggles before we are inside the moment when we are allowed to

sufficient or not. The enforcement of passports is rooted in an exclusion—a declaration

sometimes made fun of—because my accent is otherwise almost nonexistent—it is

the -ee in "refugee." In English there are many. I cannot easily control the difference

want to say "live."

mean that only one version of this reality is possible. We cannot read much into stamps.

I stand on the beach of Varosha, an empty Cypriot seaside resort. Fences and armed

when the Turkish military invaded in 1974 that for months one could see the glow

or left unclear. The Turkish authorities block all access to the town in the interest

the buildings on the other side of the fence—all looks as it should at first glance, but

promenade, storefronts with their outdated lettering, bombed-out elevator shafts. And

here and over the sea is the beach I came from. It is possible that in '74 those who had

they had little time to contemplate. Thirty years before the invasion, the British built a

the waves they too felt this sense of waiting in between the land they left and the land

north of the fence a contemporary seaside resort's speaker system is blasting techno

When I see a border agent flip through my passport behind the shatterproof glass I

the narrative sorts itself out. I imagine for some reason that at that moment they know

be innocent, since transgression is inevitable. But the truth is that that information is

an empty space large enough to accommodate their particular stamp.

I go to a Cypriot barber whose shop is across from my apartment. Before the war this

turns it into a dead end. The infrastructure of Nicosia's old city suggests forward

metal barrels I can still see the crumbling houses inside the Buffer Zone separating

customer walks in. Something about the way he waits reminds me of my grandfather.

and feel his hands running through my hair. The skin of his fingers is dry and smooth.

sitting and watching over me when I was much younger.

Turkish guards prevent any access to the town. They say it was abandoned so quickly
of television sets in the empty windows. Early looters reported family tables still set
of maintaining it as a bargaining chip for future peace negotiations. I look toward
then the cracks begin to show: untrimmed trees breaking the concrete slabs of the
no movement of people—only the breeze thrashing branches and trash. Southeast of
to depart their homes never to return were looking in the same direction, but likely
prison camp here for Jewish refugees. It is possible that when those refugees watched
they could only imagine. But perhaps they had no access to this view. Twenty meters
music and tourists are sunning themselves.

imagine they are examining the stamps, quickly allowing inked dates to fall into place as
everything I did and thought on whatever journey I was on, and so I can never truly
revealed as soon as they scan the barcode on the side. They are simply searching for

street was the main thoroughfare and now that the city is divided a wall of sandbags
motion, but this is no longer possible. If I look through the razor wire and stacked
one side from the other. Every morning I see the barber sitting inside his shop until a
I do not speak much Greek, so we remain silent. As I sit in the chair, I close my eyes
His movements are precise and patient and remind me of the feeling of my grandfather

The doorway at the bottom of the stairs is always dark, even as the sun bleaches everything above it. I have never been inside the kibbutz archive, though hidden between the collected ephemera of the community is my image repeated many times over: dressed as a monkey for Purim, dancing for the camera in a gas mask during the First Gulf War, caught brushing away soap bubbles from my first lover's face during the kibbutz carnival. The community is digitizing this documantation—transferring these moments online, where it appears their gradual decay has been arrested— the photographs no longer yellowing, the magnetic particles of the tapes ceasing to lose their charge.

FRAGMENT | FRAGMENT

What is no longer there—one body [We know there are microbiomes and halos of bacteria extending beyond our skin | We are learning about quantum mechanics | About the porousness of what seems solid] Form strapped with explosives [Bones | Muscles | Viscera | Skin | Hair | TNT | Shrapnel] Here we think is the beginning and end of the detonatorg [A fusion of human and machine | Body and explosives | At the moment of detonation]

ONE. TWO. THREE. FOUR. FIVE. SIX.

I walked parallel to ruined structures [Ruins suggest former forms | A failure to divide inside and outside] Out of the corner of my eye noting blackened materials [The heat of the explosion causing ash | Fractured glass one side of a bus station] Rubble that rolls like a landscape [The shredded innards of a restaurant | Sbarro Pizza | Mike's Place | Aroma Café] Yellow tape [Bureaucracy attempting to recreate an outside where there is no longer an inside] There are many more places I saw than places I remember seeing [And more bodies | There are few boundaries separating one from the other]

SEVEN. EIGHT. NINE. TEN. ELEVEN. TWELVE.

She is in my roommate Shai's bed [Perpendicular to mine] We are "taking a nap" [I am not asleep | My body is stiller than sleep] I do not know how to make my desire for her known [I imagine desire is an animal | Pacing with desperation | Hoping maybe she feels it too | Then our shared hunger might collapse our two bodies together]

THIRTEEN. FOURTEEN. FIFTEEN. SIXTEEN. SEVENTEEN. BOOM

Look at a landscape [The graves making up the Mount of Olives] The image lies before you flat and whole [White barren rocks | Some shaped | Some not | Some with black

lettering | Some smoothed out | Some have been here for over three thousand years]
Nothing sticks out [Pick a single grave if your sight is so good | It is no longer a land-
scape] What makes a fragment a fragment is its inability to blend with the background
[Force a piece to fit | You lose the whole]

NINETEEN. TWENTY. TWENTY-ONE. TWENTY-TWO. TWENTY-THREE.
TWENTY-FOUR.

This method of desire does not appear to work [Our bodies are not drawn together]
What becomes apparent is that I have been wearing the same pair of socks for a
week [I peeled them on and off | Never noting their sameness until now] The smell
emanating out of a pair of shoes located midhypotenuse in the triangle of our beds
[Unmistakable | Unstoppable] I ran out of socks, by error of calculation or oversight,
and I do not have laundry detergent, so I just wear the same pair [Again and again]
There they are stuffed into a pair of dirty brown suede sneakers [One and a half sizes
too large hand-me-downs | From my second cousin who is a Nike representative in
Israel] Perfuming the dorm room [Forcing me to consider what can be sensed and
what cannot]

TWENTY-FIVE. TWENTY-SIX. TWENTY-SEVEN. TWENTY-EIGHT. TWENTY-
NINE. THIRTY.

I take the bus home [The boarding school is still not home] There is a rhythm to the
Jerusalem central bus station [Beggars banging plastic cups against asphalt | Change
shaking | A vendor calling out Bageleh! Bageleh! Bageleh! | Buses that tremble when
the drivers ignite the engines] I go in and out of sleep for most of the three-hour ride
[Hopefully there is a window to lean against | Not too greasy from other human heads]
The only interruption when we all have to disembark onto a stretch of gravel before the
bus reaches Ben Gurion Airport [Our bags are all pulled out and each passenger has to
stand next to a piece of luggage to prove to the bored soldiers there are no unclaimed
suspicious ones | I think of them as wayward children]

THIRTY-ONE. THIRTY-TWO. THIRTY-THREE. THIRTY-FOUR. THIRTY-FIVE.
BOOM

Counting to eighteen [The boom is an interruption | The boom surprises | While at the same time forming a rhythm]

THIRTY-SEVEN. THIRTY-EIGHT. THIRTY-NINE. FORTY. FORTY-ONE.
FORTY-TWO.

The bus swings sharply into the Beit Lid station and this signals ten minutes to my stop [When I was little my mother and I would return this way from the hospital | I always fell asleep | My mother usually did too, and I was worried that we would miss our stop | She said, *Remember the Beit Lid stop, the turn always wakes me, don't worry*]

FORTY-THREE. FORTY-FOUR. FORTY-FIVE. FORTY-SIX. FORTY-SEVEN.
FORTY-EIGHT.

Shai and I develop a version of an old children's game [We call it EIGHTEEN BOOM | We live in room number 18 | The 18 bus is the one always blown up on its way to the boarding school] In the game we take turns counting and replacing multiples of eighteen with the word BOOM [It takes a long time for the game to grow old]

FORTY-NINE. FIFTY. FIFTY-ONE. FIFTY-TWO. FIFTY-THREE. BOOM

The Beit Lid intersection is infamous [One body detonated inside the tiny rest stop | When all the bodies still mobile rushed out a second body detonated between them | It was the first double explosion] Beit Lid is right next to the old highway on the way home [If I look west I see the security prison for Palestinians | If I look east I see the military police training base | If I look beyond the base I see the hills of the West Bank] Where I stand Israel is less than fifteen kilometers wide [They left the rubble there surrounded by yellow tape for a long time | They did not build a new rest stop]

FIFTY-FIVE. FIFTY-SIX. FIFTY-SEVEN. FIFTY-EIGHT. FIFTY-NINE. SIXTY.

In room 18 the window overlooks the Biblical Zoo [We cannot see any of the animals | We can hear the sound of the lions mating all day and all night]

SIXTY-ONE. SIXTY-TWO. SIXTY-THREE. SIXTY-FOUR. SIXTY-FIVE. SIXTY-SIX.

Our problems center on reconstruction [What to put back together] To have survived in those times does not mean I carried any marks forward [As far as detonations go my body came out unscathed | I bring no traces of explosives with me] I could note a bit of gunpowder where I forgot to scrub after returning my M-16 to the weapons' shed [That is a different substance | From a different time] Reconstruction might be necessary for people who were not unscathed [My cousin's brother-in-law | Friends from high school | People from my kibbutz] But why pull at all [Why not let those fragments disperse at their given speed and find their resting place undisturbed]

SIXTY-SEVEN. SIXTY-EIGHT. SIXTY-NINE. SEVENTY. SEVENTY-ONE. **BOOM**

Certain statements remain true with or without reconstruction [I never kissed her | I never saw an explosion | I never looked into her eyes and said anything deep | I never saw blood coming out of a body | Except in the news | I did note stains on a pavement] Certain statements start to fail the more we reconstruct [An explosion in Jerusalem | Mahene Yehuda Market | Or the Pedestrian Mall | I heard it | Or someone else heard it | And I heard them | Or I heard it on the news | Being near near death is not being near death is not being dead | I touched her hair, at least once, and that's as close as we got]

SEVENTY-THREE. SEVENTY-FOUR. SEVENTY-FIVE. SEVENTY-SIX. SEVENTY-SEVEN. SEVENTY-EIGHT.

An explosion pushes fragments from the epicenter outward [Reconstruction requires retracing the trajectory from the periphery to the core | A linear motion] Do not get stuck in the loops of what one social scientist calls Israeli media's "disaster marathon" [The postbombing news coverage on TV always showed people running in a loop | In the marketplace holding bloody rags to their face between exploded heads of cabbage]

SEVENTY-NINE. EIGHTY. EIGHTY-ONE. EIGHTY-TWO. EIGHTY-THREE. EIGHTY-FOUR.

To open up an explosion is not a difficult task [An explosion is all about opening up] It is much harder to figure out where to direct our attention [Which fragment to follow] By impulse we try to focus on one event over another [The moment of detonation | The epicenter | Bodies splitting apart | Their fragments carried by a wave too strong]

EIGHTY-FIVE. EIGHTY-SIX. EIGHTY-SEVEN. EIGHTY-EIGHT. EIGHTY-NINE. BOOM

Is there any difference between human bodies and inanimate objects when the waves stop, when force is no longer there [Our minds seem to say the objects will cease moving | Powerless | But human bodies rock back and forth | Why] The receding wave of the Mediterranean flips the speckled shell over and over [Its fan shape leaves imprints in the soaked sand | Tiny air bubbles form on the surface where the grains and sea meet | But once the wave is gone | Once even the wet outline in the sand recedes | The shell appears still]

NINETY-ONE. NINETY-TWO. NINETY-THREE. NINETY-FOUR. NINETY-FIVE. NINETY-SIX.

The narrowest part of Israel is only fifteen kilometers wide and my kibbutz was built right in the middle [Between the Mediterranean in the west and the West Bank in the east | If the communal cars have not all been checked out I can get to the beach in under fifteen minutes] I allow myself to drift out with the water [Not too far | At regular intervals making sure my feet can touch the bottom] It is difficult to keep the water from entering my body [For a few moments at least | Even in unpredictable wave forms | My limbs and back can conform to the ripples | I lose direction | If my eyes are closed] After I get out of the water I feel the waves all day long [Does the shell on the dashboard | Taken from the beach | Wave]

NINETY-SEVEN. NINETY-EIGHT. NINETY-NINE. ONE-HUNDRED. ONE-HUNDRED-AND-ONE. ONE-HUNDRED-AND-TWO.

What does a teenager do after a bombing [Suicide | Or otherwise] If you say *calls everyone they know to make sure they are safe* you might be wrong [The line at the payphone is too long] Instead the teenager searches for a blank cassette tape [Sets the radio to any Hebrew station | Hits record] The usual pop hits are interrupted with sad old ballads [A genre called "good old Israel music" | We call it "bombing attack music"] Songs like "Your Brow Is Crowned" or "Because Man Is a Tree of the Field" [ואני לא יודע | כמו האדם הוא נשרף באש | כמו העץ הוא שואף למעלה | כי האדם עץ השדה | טעמתי מזה ומזה | אהבתי וגם שנאתי | כמו עץ השדה | איפה הייתי ואיפה אהיה | כמו עץ השדה | ומר לי מר לי בפה | קברו אותי בחלקה של עפר]

ONE-HUNDRED-AND-THREE. ONE-HUNDRED-AND-FOUR. ONE-HUNDRED-AND-FIVE. ONE-HUNDRED-AND-SIX. ONE-HUNDRED-AND-SEVEN. **BOOM**

We mourn the deaths of those on this side of the fence [We also mourn the deaths of the detonatorgs | whether we want to or not]

ONE-HUNDRED-AND-NINE. ONE-HUNDRED-AND-TEN. ONE-HUNDRED-AND-ELEVEN. ONE-HUNDRED-AND-TWELVE. ONE-HUNDRED-AND-THIRTEEN. ONE-HUNDRED-AND-FOURTEEN.

For a time one of my jobs was to facilitate the hunt for these bodies before detonation [This was in a different time | This was a different substance]

ONE-HUNDRED-AND-FIFTEEN. ONE-HUNDRED-AND-SIXTEEN. ONE-HUNDRED-AND-SEVENTEEN. ONE-HUNDRED-AND-EIGHTEEN. ONE-HUNDRED-AND-NINETEEN. ONE-HUNDRED-AND-TWENTY.

I sit in my parents' living room [I watch the shaky camera running along with the crowd dispersing | I do not wake my parents up because they will find out about the explosion in the morning | I sit there with the TV on mute and I watch]

ONE-HUNDRED-AND-TWENTY-ONE. ONE-HUNDRED-AND-TWENTY-TWO. ONE-HUNDRED-AND-TWENTY-THREE. ONE-HUNDRED-AND-TWENTY-FOUR. ONE-HUNDRED-AND-TWENTY-FIVE. **BOOM**

I heard one explosion in Jerusalem [I may have reconstructed the sound] I have never been injured by this [It is safe to say my body has not been touched by shards | Not ripped to shreds | Not put together again | The same cannot be said for memory]

ONE-HUNDRED-AND-TWENTY-SEVEN. ONE-HUNDRED-AND-TWENTY-EIGHT. ONE-HUNDRED-AND-TWENTY-NINE. ONE-HUNDRED-AND-THIRTY. ONE-HUNDRED-AND-THIRTY-ONE. ONE-HUNDRED-AND-THIRTY-TWO.

I was never close to the explosion [I was close to the television screen | The television screen did not show the explosion | It showed what happened after]

ONE-HUNDRED-AND-THIRTY-THREE. ONE-HUNDRED-AND-THIRTY-FOUR. ONE-HUNDRED-AND-THIRTY-FIVE. ONE-HUNDRED-AND-THIRTY-SIX. ONE-HUNDRED-AND-THIRTY-SEVEN. ONE-HUNDRED-AND-THIRTY-EIGHT.

I sit close to the television screen and watch [There are captions indicating the location and the number of dead | They do not have names yet] Obviously this is not my body running [My body should be asleep | These events interrupt my time] It may seem cruel to think about this as an interruption as if the explosion was not important in itself [It is not like I have a story about the time I did not kiss the girl because an explosion tore us apart | I did not kiss the girl because I was too shy | I remember her asking me to run my hands through her hair | Taking out my retainer and slipping it into my coat pocket | Just in case]

ONE-HUNDRED-AND-THIRTY-NINE. ONE-HUNDRED-AND-FORTY. ONE-HUNDRED-AND-FORTY-ONE. ONE-HUNDRED-AND-FORTY-TWO. ONE-HUNDRED-AND-FORTY-THREE. **BOOM**

She nearly missed an explosion on the bus one day in downtown Jerusalem [We did not kiss in the neighborhood above the boarding school | Not when she placed her head in my lap on the bench by the supermarket | Not while we were sitting on the boulders in the empty hill between the economically depressed immigrant housing project and the school | We did not kiss even though I took out my retainer and slipped it into my coat pocket where it got covered in lint]

ONE-HUNDRED-AND-FORTY-FIVE. ONE-HUNDRED-AND-FORTY-SIX. ONE-HUNDRED-AND-FORTY-SEVEN. ONE-HUNDRED-AND-FORTY-EIGHT. ONE-HUNDRED-AND-FORTY-NINE. ONE-HUNDRED-AND-FIFTY.

It would be more dramatic to say that the kiss was interrupted by an explosion [It was not |It was because I was too shy | We did not kiss then | I never kissed the girl who was near the explosion]

ONE-HUNDRED-AND-FIFTY-ONE. ONE-HUNDRED-AND-FIFTY-TWO. ONE-HUNDRED-AND-FIFTY-THREE. ONE-HUNDRED-AND-FIFTY-FOUR. ONE-HUNDRED-AND-FIFTY-FIVE. ONE-HUNDRED-AND-FIFTY-SIX.

For her high school graduation art show she had us all sit in the school screening room where she showed us her film [The camera was her eye | She was running in the fields outside the house where she grew up | The camera was shaky | Her puffy silver jacket was rustling | The camera was pointing to the side | She was breathing hard from the running | The fields were passing parallel to the camera | She kept running and running] She strapped egg cartons covered with cellophane to all of the seats [When we moved the seats made loud noises | Hundreds of little crinkles] By then it was much too late for me to kiss her [Nothing happened to her | She was just near the explosion | When she came back to school our friends said *She was near the explosion* | That was it | The crinkles made moving very uncomfortable]

ONE-HUNDRED-AND-FIFTY-SEVEN. ONE-HUNDRED-AND-FIFTY-EIGHT. ONE-HUNDRED-AND-FIFTY-NINE. ONE-HUNDRED-AND-SIXTY. ONE-HUNDRED-AND-SIXTY-ONE. **BOOM**

I do not remember being afraid of blowing up [Maybe it was that teenage pretend-fearlessness] We used to sneak into Mike's Place [A bar in the Russian Compound near the Old City | It catered mostly to tourists | The bouncer did not check IDs] The place was crowded and a little steamy [Compared with the cold outside] Mike's Place blew up [Not when we were there]

ONE-HUNDRED-AND-SIXTY-THREE. ONE-HUNDRED-AND-SIXTY-FOUR. ONE-HUNDRED-AND-SIXTY-FIVE. ONE-HUNDRED-AND-SIXTY-SIX. ONE-HUNDRED-AND-SIXTY-SEVEN. ONE-HUNDRED-AND-SIXTY-EIGHT.

It was very uncomfortable to watch the movie [Every time one of us shifted we would make crinkling noises] It was clear the girl who was near the explosion was showing us something intimate [The camera pointing where she was looking | The camera moving as her body was moving | The fields running parallel | Inescapable] When we moved the crinkles kept interrupting [She wanted us to know she knew we were watching]

ONE-HUNDRED-AND-SIXTY-NINE. ONE-HUNDRED-AND-SEVENTY. ONE-HUNDRED-AND-SEVENTY-ONE. ONE-HUNDRED-AND-SEVENTY-TWO. ONE-HUNDRED-AND-SEVENTY-THREE. ONE-HUNDRED-AND-SEVENTY-FOUR.

There was no explosion in the film made by the girl who was near the explosion [The cellophane made many small detonations]

ONE-HUNDRED-AND-SEVENTY-FIVE. ONE-HUNDRED-AND-SEVENTY-SIX. ONE-HUNDRED-AND-SEVENTY-SEVEN. ONE-HUNDRED-AND-SEVENTY-EIGHT. ONE-HUNDRED-AND-SEVENTY-NINE. BOOM

I talk about the not-kissing and the explosions because they both happened at the same time [Not because not-kissing felt like an explosion at the time]

ONE-HUNDRED-AND-EIGHTY-ONE. ONE-HUNDRED-AND-EIGHTY-TWO. ONE-HUNDRED-AND-EIGHTY-THREE. ONE-HUNDRED-AND-EIGHTY-FOUR. ONE-HUNDRED-AND-EIGHTY-FIVE. ONE-HUNDRED-AND-EIGHTY-SIX.

After the explosion there is a common ritual [Eventually someone takes responsibility | Ambulances and police forces arrive | They collect and remove the people | The people are scattering in all directions and they must be removed] ZAKA (Disaster Victim Identification) volunteers arrive and collect the bodies [They are the most concerned about the fragments | They move about the scene collecting every bit of human flesh and blood | Body parts must be buried with the right body | If there is enough of one left | Otherwise | If there is no body left | It is just a large collection of fragments] Can we live with that [As long as the parts are all together | It is the Jewish custom to bury every single bit | It must be observed] ZAKA are the most observant [They know about the dispersal of fragments | They do the best job of reconstructing | It is their responsibility to make sure the fragments do not become part of the landscape]

ONE-HUNDRED-AND-EIGHTY-SEVEN. ONE-HUNDRED-AND-EIGHTY-EIGHT. ONE-HUNDRED-AND-EIGHTY-NINE. ONE-HUNDRED-AND-NINETY. ONE-HUNDRED-AND-NINETY-ONE. ONE-HUNDRED-AND-NINETY-TWO.

It is possible I am overcomplicating the explosion [It happened and all particles moved forward from the core and no return is possible to the moment before]

ONE-HUNDRED-AND-NINETY-THREE. ONE-HUNDRED-AND-NINETY-FOUR. ONE-HUNDRED-AND-NINETY-FIVE. ONE-HUNDRED-AND-NINETY-SIX. ONE-HUNDRED-AND-NINETY-SEVEN. **BOOM**

The moment following the explosion becomes much easier than the moment before the explosion [After the first several experiences of everyday detonations | They do provide a training of sorts | Not quite rehearsals] Finally all that potential energy is expressed [When I sat at the front of the bus and caught the radio announcer interrupting regular programming | I exhaled | I realized I had been holding my breath for so long] My grandfather said that once the Soviets invaded Estonia everything fell into place [He could relax because he knew what was coming | He did not know what was coming]

ONE-HUNDRED-AND-NINETY-NINE. TWO-HUNDRED. TWO-HUNDRED-AND-ONE. TWO-HUNDRED-AND-TWO. TWO-HUNDRED-AND-THREE. TWO-HUNDRED-AND-FOUR.

There is a difference between everyday explosions and those in times of war [We were sitting in my grandparents' living room when the sirens sounded | Distant | Then closer | The rockets from Lebanon had never reached this far south | We looked at each other | We walked outside | We looked at the sky | We saw nothing | We heard an explosion | We could not place it | Is that what a rocket sounds like I asked him | Is the nearest bomb shelter the gym he asked me | We walked to the gym which is next to the kibbutz pool | It was open and ready for shelter | There were mirrors for gym-goers to look at themselves exercising | Mirrors in which my father and I were not looking | We knew we would see each other]

TWO-HUNDRED-AND-FIVE. TWO-HUNDRED-AND-SIX. TWO-HUNDRED-AND-SEVEN. TWO-HUNDRED-AND-EIGHT. TWO-HUNDRED-AND-NINE. TWO-HUNDRED-AND-TEN.

They tell me Scud missiles launched from Iraq chart their course across the sky like a cigarette tossed from the top of a building [Little red flame] Those who tell me this have fathers who take them to the rooftops at night whenever the sirens sound [They sit in plastic lawn chairs and watch the eastern horizon | My family goes straight to the Sealed Room where we put gas masks over our heads and watch each other]

TWO-HUNDRED-AND-ELEVEN. TWO-HUNDRED-AND-TWELVE. TWO-HUNDRED-AND-THIRTEEN. TWO-HUNDRED-AND-FOURTEEN. TWO-HUNDRED-AND-FIFTEEN. **BOOM**

Most of the everyday explosions were a secondhand experience [I draw a line from the epicenters to me | From the TV to me | From the wounded to me | I wonder what reaches | All the way from the city]

TWO-HUNDRED-AND-SEVENTEEN. TWO-HUNDRED-AND-EIGHTEEN. TWO-HUNDRED-AND-NINETEEN. TWO-HUNDRED-AND-TWENTY. TWO-HUNDRED-AND-TWENTY-ONE. TWO-HUNDRED-AND-TWENTY-TWO.

It is easy to be in the proximity of explosions when there are many explosions [I find it necessary to remind myself that at the center of the detonations is a human body | Strapped with explosives]

TWO-HUNDRED-AND-TWENTY-THREE. TWO-HUNDRED-AND-TWENTY-FOUR. TWO-HUNDRED-AND-TWENTY-FIVE. TWO-HUNDRED-AND-TWENTY-SIX. TWO-HUNDRED-AND-TWENTY-SEVEN. TWO-HUNDRED-AND-TWENTY-EIGHT.

[In his last testament he said] How beautiful for the splinters of my bones to be the response that blows up the enemy | Not for the love of killing | So we can live as other people live | We do not sing the songs of death | We recite the hymns of life | We die so that future generations may live [In his last testament he said]

TWO-HUNDRED-AND-TWENTY-NINE. TWO-HUNDRED-AND-THIRTY. TWO-HUNDRED-AND-THIRTY-ONE. TWO-HUNDRED-AND-THIRTY-TWO. TWO-HUNDRED-AND-THIRTY-THREE. **BOOM**

Would the process of fragment reconstruction change if the moment of detonation was an act of love [Hate might be easier to impose] Can I blame detonatorgs for claiming their agency through one of the only political rituals still available in this world of ours [Who can say we are all not in one way or another participating in the inclusion of others in the damage we do to ourselves]

TWO-HUNDRED-AND-THIRTY-FIVE. TWO-HUNDRED-AND-THIRTY-SIX. TWO-HUNDRED-AND-THIRTY-SEVEN. TWO-HUNDRED-AND-THIRTY-EIGHT. TWO-HUNDRED-AND-THIRTY-NINE. TWO-HUNDRED-AND-FORTY.

On this side of the fence we call it *pigooah hitabdoot* (suicide attack) [This means there is an attack and a suicide] On the other side of the fence there are different words [Not *tafjirat intihariyya* (suicide bombing) | Instead *amaliyat istishhadiyya* (martyrdom operation)] The organizations that carry out these attacks insist on the difference [One is an escape | The other sacrifice] I call them detonatorgs [At the moment their decision is made | I choose to collect human and machine | I bind wire and organ together]

TWO-HUNDRED-AND-FORTY-ONE. TWO-HUNDRED-AND-FORTY-TWO. TWO-HUNDRED-AND-FORTY-THREE. TWO-HUNDRED-AND-FORTY-FOUR. TWO-HUNDRED-AND-FORTY-FIVE. TWO-HUNDRED-AND-FORTY-SIX.

Can we run parallel to the fragments [Noting their speed and direction | Without causing them to loop over and over]

TWO-HUNDRED-AND-FORTY-SEVEN. TWO-HUNDRED-AND-FORTY-EIGHT. TWO-HUNDRED-AND-FORTY-NINE. TWO-HUNDRED-AND-FIFTY. TWO-HUNDRED-AND-FIFTY-ONE. **BOOM**

[He said] The power of the spirit pulls us upward | While the power of material things pulls us downward [He said] Someone bent on martyrdom becomes immune to the material pull [Their planner asked] What if the operation fails [They said] In any case | We get to meet the Prophet and his companions | *Inshallah* [They said] We were floating | Swimming | In the feeling that we were about to enter eternity [He said]

TWO-HUNDRED-AND-FIFTY-THREE. TWO-HUNDRED-AND-FIFTY-FOUR. TWO-HUNDRED-AND-FIFTY-FIVE. TWO-HUNDRED-AND-FIFTY-SIX. TWO-HUNDRED-AND-FIFTY-SEVEN. TWO-HUNDRED-AND-FIFTY-EIGHT.

To say that I was not directly exposed to explosions [Does not mean I was not averse to them | Does not mean I was not attracted to them]

TWO-HUNDRED-AND-FIFTY-NINE. TWO-HUNDRED-AND-SIXTY. TWO-HUNDRED-AND-SIXTY-ONE. TWO-HUNDRED-AND-SIXTY-TWO. TWO-HUNDRED-AND-SIXTY-THREE. TWO-HUNDRED-AND-SIXTY-FOUR.

Public transportation felt the most dangerous [It was enough to be walking by the bus | Inch forward in a car behind the bus | Cross in front of the bus | The explosion was big enough]

TWO-HUNDRED-AND-SIXTY-FIVE. TWO-HUNDRED-AND-SIXTY-SIX. TWO-HUNDRED-AND-SIXTY-SEVEN. TWO-HUNDRED-AND-SIXTY-EIGHT. TWO-HUNDRED-AND-SIXTY-NINE. **BOOM**

There are stories of survivors [The girl who took her change from the driver | The coin that slipped and fell to the floor of the bus | The coin that rolled to the back | The girl who ran after it | The bomb that exploded too far to kill | Her] Perhaps coins, like shells, carry waves [Who knows if that coin had not been in an explosion before | Money is a stubborn thing] In the truth we know [Coins | Like the dead | Do not care]

TWO-HUNDRED-AND-SEVENTY-ONE. TWO-HUNDRED-AND-SEVENTY-TWO. TWO-HUNDRED-AND-SEVENTY-THREE. TWO-HUNDRED-AND-SEVENTY-FOUR. TWO-HUNDRED-AND-SEVENTY-FIVE. TWO-HUNDRED-AND-SEVENTY-SIX.

[His father said] Even after Salah saw my son ripped to shreds | He did not flinch | He waited before exploding himself | in order to cause additional deaths [His father said]

TWO-HUNDRED-AND-SEVENTY-SEVEN. TWO-HUNDRED-AND-SEVENTY-EIGHT. TWO-HUNDRED-AND-SEVENTY-NINE. TWO-HUNDRED-AND-EIGHTY. TWO-HUNDRED-AND-EIGHTY-ONE. TWO-HUNDRED-AND-EIGHTY-TWO.

If the shell does not feel the waves anymore [What then] I want to think that its atoms remember the waves [That it too rocked back and forth | Back and forth] In Beit Lid by the bus station there was an improvised memorial for the people who died in the explosion [The two who detonated were not included | Though like mourning | The memorial commemorates them | Whether we want it to or not] The improvised memorial was made of a rusted mortar shell etched with the names of the dead [Surrounded by upright metal leaves | one for each dead]

TWO-HUNDRED-AND-EIGHTY-THREE. TWO-HUNDRED-AND-EIGHTY-FOUR. TWO-HUNDRED-AND-EIGHTY-FIVE. TWO-HUNDRED-AND-EIGHTY-SIX. TWO-HUNDRED-AND-EIGHTY-SEVEN. **BOOM**

[They said] His soul was borne upward | On a fragment of the bomb [They said]

TWO-HUNDRED-AND-EIGHTY-NINE. TWO-HUNDRED-AND-NINETY. TWO-HUNDRED-AND-NINETY-ONE. TWO-HUNDRED-AND-NINETY-TWO. TWO-HUNDRED-AND-NINETY-THREE. TWO-HUNDRED-AND-NINETY-FOUR.

Years later the memorial was removed [Memorial | Not memory] A new one was built five hundred meters east of the site of the explosion [Larger | Commissioned | Not improvised] The new fenced-in memorial is made of nineteen metal human figures ascending a staircase leading nowhere [Their bodies hunched | As if the earth was pulling them down | While trying to ascend]

TWO-HUNDRED-AND-NINETY-FIVE. TWO-HUNDRED-AND-NINETY-SIX. TWO-HUNDRED-AND-NINETY-SEVEN. TWO-HUNDRED-AND-NINETY-EIGHT. TWO-HUNDRED-AND-NINETY-NINE. THREE-HUNDRED.

Even though I was not there I can still see the two bodies exploding in Beit Lid in my mind [As these fragments show I may not remember things I have seen | As these fragments show I may remember things I have not seen] So we are all good [Living is forgetting | Is remembering]

THREE-HUNDRED-AND-ONE. THREE-HUNDRED-AND-TWO. THREE-HUNDRED-AND-THREE. THREE-HUNDRED-AND-FOUR. THREE-HUNDRED-AND-FIVE. **BOOM**

When I thought about sex I mostly thought about being tired in someone else's arms [Not the explosive climax] If you are in pieces you do not get to be tired in someone else's arms [It is true that according to Jewish custom your pieces will be picked up by someone else's arms]

THREE-HUNDRED-AND-SEVEN. THREE-HUNDRED-AND-EIGHT. THREE-HUNDRED-AND-NINE. THREE-HUNDRED-AND-TEN. THREE-HUNDRED-AND-ELEVEN. THREE-HUNDRED-AND-TWELVE.

What I cannot forget is the first day of military service [The soldierization chain | Winding in a loop inside the main recruitment base] I was told I entered a building as a civilian and exited a soldier [My body property of the state] There were lines in which to wait [It was hard to remove the ink used to take fingerprints | It was hard to accommodate the metal square inside the mouth to take the dental photo | It was hard to be told to put one of our dog tags into a special pocket in our boot in order to make it easier to identify our foot in case it blows off] These are fragments too [Though perhaps made of a different substance]

THREE-HUNDRED-AND-THIRTEEN. THREE-HUNDRED-AND-FOURTEEN. THREE-HUNDRED-AND-FIFTEEN. THREE-HUNDRED-AND-SIXTEEN. THREE-HUNDRED-AND-SEVENTEEN. THREE-HUNDRED-AND-EIGHTEEN.

ZAKA's gathering appears to exist in opposition to the acts of detonatorgs [They pass through the ruins | Pulling fragments together | From the epicenter that was the detonatorg] The danger of a second detonation is always present [Always the risk of rescuer becoming victim | Always the risk of a second epicenter] ZAKA volunteers are not that different from detonatorgs [Though the movement of the fragments is reversed] Both agents operate under a religious ideology [An imposition of the sacred on public sacrificial death]

THREE-HUNDRED-AND-NINETEEN. THREE-HUNDRED-AND-TWENTY. THREE-HUNDRED-AND-TWENTY-ONE. THREE-HUNDRED-AND-TWENTY-TWO. THREE-HUNDRED-AND-TWENTY-THREE. BOOM

I was about to board a bus in the terminal when the passengers began to disembark [We were at the point of origin | No one had arrived where they were going] [An old man turned to me and said] There is a scary-looking Palestinian on the bus | You're a soldier, take him off [An old man said] I did not know what to say to that [I boarded the bus and sat down]

THREE-HUNDRED-AND-TWENTY-FIVE. THREE-HUNDRED-AND-TWENTY-SIX. THREE-HUNDRED-AND-TWENTY-SEVEN. THREE-HUNDRED-AND-TWENTY-EIGHT. THREE-HUNDRED-AND-TWENTY-NINE. THREE-HUNDRED-AND-THIRTY.

The first detonatorgs here were not Arab Palestinians [They were two Jewish men sentenced to death | Members of the right-wing militant underground when the British ruled here] Rather than allowing the British military to execute them they chose suicide [Or was it heroism | Some cast them as Samsons] They embraced an orange between their hearts [And blew themselves apart]

THREE-HUNDRED-AND-THIRTY-ONE. THREE-HUNDRED-AND-THIRTY-TWO. THREE-HUNDRED-AND-THIRTY-THREE. THREE-HUNDRED-AND-THIRTY-FOUR. THREE-HUNDRED-AND-THIRTY-FIVE. THREE-HUNDRED-AND-THIRTY-SIX.

The detonatorgs do not speak [The recordings | The testaments | Released after the explosions are of humans | Not detonatorgs | They are not detonatorgs until they detonate] It is a feature of detonatorgs that others speak for them [Their peers | Their families | Their former selves | Strangers]

THREE-HUNDRED-AND-THIRTY-SEVEN. THREE-HUNDRED-AND-THIRTY-EIGHT. THREE-HUNDRED-AND-THIRTY-NINE. THREE-HUNDRED-AND-FORTY. THREE-HUNDRED-AND-FORTY-ONE. **BOOM**

Twenty-five years after the event the engineer who made the orange grenades receives a phone call [The brother of one of those first detonatorgs invites the engineer to a wedding | This man's father does not have many more years to live and the father wants to meet the engineer and *exchange a few words*] The engineer does not want to come to the wedding [Does not want to see the detonatorg's father] The detonatorg's brother says [*You can't escape this*] The brother says [*You owe this to us | My father's wish is for me a command*] The engineer tries to get out of the wedding [They insist | They even move the wedding from Jerusalem to a banquet hall near the engineer's house in Ramat Gan]

THREE-HUNDRED-AND-FORTY-THREE. THREE-HUNDRED-AND-FORTY-FOUR. THREE-HUNDRED-AND-FORTY-FIVE. THREE-HUNDRED-AND-

FORTY-SIX. THREE-HUNDRED-AND-FORTY-SEVEN. THREE-HUNDRED-AND-FORTY-EIGHT.

When the engineer finally arrives at the wedding the detonatorg's brother sees him [The brother says, *Oh! So glad you came* | *Wait here and I will fetch my father*] The old man, the father, kisses and hugs the engineer and says, *You saved the honor of Israel* [The engineer is crying] The engineer says [*Dear rabbi* | *It's not me* | *It's your son* | *I did nothing*] The father says [*Yes* | *This is true* | *But were it not for your construction he could not have done it*] The engineer is surprised by his feelings [The engineer is crying] The father says [*If you did not construct it for him he wouldn't have been able to do it* | *He would have been hung like a lowly criminal*] This changed the engineer's feelings [About the morality of what he did]

THREE-HUNDRED-AND-FORTY-NINE. THREE-HUNDRED-AND-FIFTY. THREE-HUNDRED-AND-FIFTY-ONE. THREE-HUNDRED-AND-FIFTY-TWO. THREE-HUNDRED-AND-FIFTY-THREE. THREE-HUNDRED-AND-FIFTY-FOUR.

[Fifty years later the engineer who made the oranges says] Journalists and reporters criticize me for enabling their suicide | It was not suicide at all | It was a military operation | The suicide was a way for them to teach | Sacrifice | Dedication | Heroism | What is a higher goal for a warrior than this [Fifty years later the engineer who made the oranges said]

THREE-HUNDRED-AND-FIFTY-FIVE. THREE-HUNDRED-AND-FIFTY-SIX. THREE-HUNDRED-AND-FIFTY-SEVEN. THREE-HUNDRED-AND-FIFTY-EIGHT. THREE-HUNDRED-AND-FIFTY-NINE. **BOOM**

If only I thought the collection of fragments was an act imbued with divine will [Forgive me for not including more of the divine] Perhaps reconstruction is not such a problem [It is true that the struggle over this place is often attached to divine right | That the right of a human to inflict pain on others is given to them from god] In these fragments I do not know if we are from dust [If we will return]

THREE-HUNDRED-AND-SIXTY-ONE. THREE-HUNDRED-AND-SIXTY-TWO. THREE-HUNDRED-AND-SIXTY-THREE. THREE-HUNDRED-AND-SIXTY-FOUR. THREE-HUNDRED-AND-SIXTY-FIVE. THREE-HUNDRED-AND-SIXTY-SIX.

On television the people are running [In a loop] In newspapers the editors satisfy us with pictures [Of the charred skeleton | Of a bus] Images are not enough [It is important to engage the other senses with descriptions of sounds | Of smells | Of the body] Buses cannot feel [That does not mean I cannot stare at the empty cavities of the headlights and think that the bus looks exhausted] I do not see the explosions on the other side of the fence [Those that are not aimed at me | Those that are done in my collective name] I do not see the explosions on this side of the fence [Only the loop on the television]

THREE-HUNDRED-AND-SIXTY-SEVEN. THREE-HUNDRED-AND-SIXTY-EIGHT. THREE-HUNDRED-AND-SIXTY-NINE. THREE-HUNDRED-AND-SEVENTY. THREE-HUNDRED-AND-SEVENTY-ONE. THREE-HUNDRED-AND-SEVENTY-TWO.

Since when does a place belong to anyone [We live and we die and the place stays]

THREE-HUNDRED-AND-SEVENTY-THREE. THREE-HUNDRED-AND-SEVENTY-FOUR. THREE-HUNDRED-AND-SEVENTY-FIVE. THREE-HUNDRED-AND-SEVENTY-SIX. THREE-HUNDRED-AND-SEVENTY-SEVEN. **BOOM**

I can pull the fragments together again and again [This does not make the body whole]

THREE-HUNDRED-AND-SEVENTY-NINE. THREE-HUNDRED-AND-EIGHTY. THREE-HUNDRED-AND-EIGHTY-ONE. THREE-HUNDRED-AND-EIGHTY-TWO. THREE-HUNDRED-AND-EIGHTY-THREE. THREE-HUNDRED-AND-EIGHTY-FOUR.

It is sad for me to think that shells do not feel the waves [When I ride back in the car after a day at the beach I cannot stop my body from rocking back and forth | Rocking back and forth even though there is no water pushing at all]

THREE-HUNDRED-AND-EIGHTY-FIVE. THREE-HUNDRED-AND-EIGHTY-SIX. THREE-HUNDRED-AND-EIGHTY-SEVEN. THREE-HUNDRED-AND-EIGHTY-EIGHT. THREE-HUNDRED-AND-EIGHTY-NINE. THREE-HUNDRED-AND-NINETY.

If the girl who was near the explosion and I ever ate together it was definitely not at a pizza shop downtown [Sbarro was near where the girl was near the explosion | Sbarro later blew up too] The news said that the suicide bomber asked how much time it would take to make spaghetti then detonated a bomb that was in a guitar case slung across his back [How the newspaper knew what he said I do not know] It would have been strange if the girl who was near the explosion and I ate at the Sbarro which later exploded [That is not the case]

THREE-HUNDRED-AND-NINETY-ONE. THREE-HUNDRED-AND-NINETY-TWO. THREE-HUNDRED-AND-NINETY-THREE. THREE-HUNDRED-AND-NINETY-FOUR. THREE-HUNDRED-AND-NINETY-FIVE. **BOOM**

There was an art exhibit in a Palestinian university celebrating the anniversary of this explosion [Plastic body parts and pizza slices were strewn across a room | A big Sbarro sign hung above] I have only read descriptions of this exhibit [I know enough to know that body parts do not rock back and forth on their own after they have flown in a line away from the epicenter and settled]

THREE-HUNDRED-AND-NINETY-SEVEN. THREE-HUNDRED-AND-NINETY-EIGHT. THREE-HUNDRED-AND-NINETY-NINE. FOUR-HUNDRED. FOUR-HUNDRED-AND-ONE. FOUR-HUNDRED-AND-TWO.

Fragments seem to suggest that there is a whole object [To put together] Perhaps the idea of anything whole is faulty to begin with [Is this different for people who think they see the whole in the act of fragmenting] There might not be anything whole there at all [Some of us might be carried forward in life by the sense that some things are whole and some things are broken]

FOUR-HUNDRED-AND-THREE. FOUR-HUNDRED-AND-FOUR. FOUR-HUNDRED-AND-FIVE. FOUR-HUNDRED-AND-SIX. FOUR-HUNDRED-AND-SEVEN. FOUR-HUNDRED-AND-EIGHT.

One year an entire flock of cranes settled in the grove of pine trees surrounding my father's studio [Hundreds of birds | Their white droppings painting the ground and discarded pine needles below] A gas cannon was brought to chase them away [It exploded every thirty minutes | We expected the boom to drive them off | Cause them to fold their long necks and search for a different grove] The loud interruption was too great [Every thirty minutes their hearts exploded inside their chests | They dropped to the ground] Those whose hearts did not explode would flee then forget and resettle in the pines [Underneath them would collect the brown pine needles | The white droppings | The bodies of their flockmates]

FOUR-HUNDRED-AND-NINE. FOUR-HUNDRED-AND-TEN. FOUR-HUNDRED-AND-ELEVEN. FOUR-HUNDRED-AND-TWELVE. FOUR-HUNDRED-AND-THIRTEEN. BOOM

There is a crane outside the window [Behind it I can see the clouds are moving | I can see they are moving because the crane is still] The crane is here to demolish the building next to the library where I am working [I do not see the crane demolishing | I only see the still crane and the still ruins] Every day I come here and look [The yellow construction machines are busy making the earth flat | I am very far from where the explosions happened]

FOUR-HUNDRED-AND-FIFTEEN. FOUR-HUNDRED-AND-SIXTEEN. FOUR-HUNDRED-AND-SEVENTEEN. FOUR-HUNDRED-AND-EIGHTEEN. FOUR-HUNDRED-AND-NINETEEN. FOUR-HUNDRED-AND-TWENTY.

Has the television loop flattened the fragment [In another time with multiple irreproducible perspectives | No one experienced the same fragment from the same angle] That would ignore how long stories have been around [As a way to stabilize a telling | Back and forth | Back and forth]

FOUR-HUNDRED-AND-TWENTY-ONE. FOUR-HUNDRED-AND-TWENTY-TWO. FOUR-HUNDRED-AND-TWENTY-THREE. FOUR-HUNDRED-AND-TWENTY-FOUR. FOUR-HUNDRED-AND-TWENTY-FIVE. FOUR-HUNDRED-AND-TWENTY-SIX.

I went to a funeral for a girl who committed suicide [I did not know her when she was alive | I did not know her when she was dead] She was the younger sister of one of my soldiers [I did not intend to become a commander | Experience pushed me that way] I did not like this soldier very much and had her transferred to another unit before her sister's suicide [After the suicide I felt guilty | The connection may not even really be there | How do we know the knocking of one event into another] It was a suicide by hanging [There were slow shuffles and subdued sobs | There were no people yelling and running in loops]

FOUR-HUNDRED-AND-TWENTY-SEVEN. FOUR-HUNDRED-AND-TWENTY-EIGHT. FOUR-HUNDRED-AND-TWENTY-NINE. FOUR-HUNDRED-AND-THIRTY. FOUR-HUNDRED-AND-THIRTY-ONE. **BOOM**

I cannot see the fragments from her family's perspective [For one human body other human bodies might just as well be shells on the beach | We cannot feel them rock back and forth | Back and forth]

FOUR-HUNDRED-AND-THIRTY-THREE. FOUR-HUNDRED-AND-THIRTY-FOUR. FOUR-HUNDRED-AND-THIRTY-FIVE. FOUR-HUNDRED-AND-THIRTY-SIX. FOUR-HUNDRED-AND-THIRTY-SEVEN. FOUR-HUNDRED-AND-THIRTY-EIGHT.

The rules change when we introduce stories [Devices that have the power to extract fragments from the landscape and contain them together | Or are they containing people]

FOUR-HUNDRED-AND-THIRTY-NINE. FOUR-HUNDRED-AND-FORTY. FOUR-HUNDRED-AND-FORTY-ONE. FOUR-HUNDRED-AND-FORTY-TWO. FOUR-HUNDRED-AND-FORTY-THREE. FOUR-HUNDRED-AND-FORTY-FOUR.

I love brushing the white sand off my feet after a day on the shoreline [Getting in the car | Feeling the waves rock me back and forth for the rest of the afternoon] If we are lucky an encounter with waves will make us remember [If unlucky the waves will break us | Perhaps it is the other way around | Luck could be an illusion of causality interpreted in hindsight] You will not hear those words cross my lips [I do not want to tempt luck]

FOUR-HUNDRED-AND-FORTY-FIVE. FOUR-HUNDRED-AND-FORTY-SIX. FOUR-HUNDRED-AND-FORTY-SEVEN. FOUR-HUNDRED-AND-FORTY-EIGHT. FOUR-HUNDRED-AND-FORTY-NINE. **BOOM**

ZAKA no longer only tend to the dead [They now respond to emergencies of the living | The living need collecting too] Their massive network allows them faster response than official ambulances and paramedics [Their worldview forms a narrative people can understand]

FOUR-HUNDRED-AND-FIFTY-ONE. FOUR-HUNDRED-AND-FIFTY-TWO. FOUR-HUNDRED-AND-FIFTY-THREE. FOUR-HUNDRED-AND-FIFTY-FOUR. FOUR-HUNDRED-AND-FIFTY-FIVE. FOUR-HUNDRED-AND-FIFTY-SIX.

I understand we are making do with fragments [Of video | Of body | Of metal scraps]
On either side we make do [The bomb a fusion of body and explosives | The fragments
a fusion of bodies and explosion] We tell ourselves stories to maintain coherency [In
a loop | In a line | In proximity] We move about the scene and collect [To approxi-
mate the before] We enumerate all we have not been touched by [Shrapnel | Fervor |
Heat | Waves]

FOUR-HUNDRED-AND-FIFTY-SEVEN. FOUR-HUNDRED-AND-FIFTY-EIGHT.
FOUR-HUNDRED-AND-FIFTY-NINE. FOUR-HUNDRED-AND-SIXTY. FOUR-
HUNDRED-AND-SIXTY-ONE. FOUR-HUNDRED-AND-SIXTY-TWO.

We expect the explosion to drive us off [The loop returns us | Our hearts do not
explode] All day we want to feel the weight of the fragments collecting [Whether they
have ascended no one can say]

FOUR-HUNDRED-AND-SIXTY-THREE. FOUR-HUNDRED-AND-SIXTY-FOUR.
FOUR-HUNDRED-AND-SIXTY-FIVE. FOUR-HUNDRED-AND-SIXTY-SIX. FOUR-
HUNDRED-AND-SIXTY-SEVEN. **BOOM**

I watch as my belongings are systematically exposed—folded clothes undone, sheets of a journal removed from their spine. I am waiting for a photograph. When I cross the border, told to move to the side of the line, I question while trying to appear nonquestioning. When taken to a locked cell and body-searched I maintain composure while in an uncustomary posture. I am waiting for a photograph to confirm I am who my passport says I am. I am waiting and accumulating exposure in this cell.

EROS
THE MULTIPLE-CHOICED
THE ALGORITHMIC
THE INTELLIGENCER
THE BITTERSWEET

Eros is a creature against whom no technology avails.
—ANNE CARSON

[In the beginning it's just exciting: so many secrets. This classified source is above TOP SECRET clearance and, even though I'm already not allowed to share any of my work, they say I have to sign a paper stating I won't reveal a single detail, or face imprisonment. They say the project is intended to verify the other side's intent, but it is clear to everyone involved that the true intention is to find as much dirt on the other side as possible.]

If my body used to slice through the night air in an unbroken stride, it was only to hide that my true interest was not in forward motion but rather to revel in the fragments inside every house seen out of the corner of the eye. There was only the light of a subdued lamp in a corner of a room, rays bouncing off the fabric of the everyday and out a single windowpane into darkness and a pupil wide enough to receive them.

Would you consider dating somebody who publishes the most intimate details of their relationships in their blog?

- Yes.
✓ No.

Your explanation
Probably not. See "intimacy," from Latin "intus–" within.

> **Let's say there are two people in a room with you; one is loud, flirty and attention getting, the other is shy and quiet. Which one are you attracted to more?**
>
> • The loud flirty one
> ✓ The shy and quiet one
>
> **Your explanation**
> Depends. Which one is closer to the cheese tray?

We are one when we know someone is watching. We are another when we think no one is. Which one is which one? We are illuminated. We cast shadows. We tighten our expression or our abdomen or pick at the frayed strands of our surface, thinking this is it. This is the image. Whole.

[The other side begins to suspect their phones are tapped, which they are. They exercise caution and refrain from making calls, but they do not realize that the phones are always transmitting whether they are on or off.]

Let the pieces stand in, and drops become a sea, blades a meadow, grains a beach. Or silver halide a photograph. Let them compose someone new and exciting. Let them become a potential with no history to shoulder.

What is the most exciting thing about getting to know someone new?

✓ Discovering your shared interests

• Discovering their body

Your explanation

Discovering your shared body, of course! Wait, that doesn't make sense. Or does it?

[I am funded by a foreign intelligence agency to translate this dirt. They provide the money rather freely since we are, after all, one of their closest allies. We do our share for them as well—as soon as we heard about the planes striking and the towers collapsing I was ordered to compose our offer of intelligence support, of condolence and promise. Later, when I found out we were the first ally to reach out, and the foreign agency's director felt personally moved, I was not so much impressed that I played a small role in history as I was embarrassed that I made a grammatical error.]

I, I, I, so sweet, so, so, so, so bitter.

Imagine that you are in an uncommitted relationship with someone you have grown to deeply care about. They begin to date someone else who seems to make them happier than you do. Which would you do?

- Bow out.
- Try harder to win their love.
- ✓ Continue as before.

Your explanation

I don't like the basic assumptions of this question that both relationships can't coexist simultaneously, and that love is winnable.

[Dirt means admissions the other side would not make in public. Dirt means plans we mean to thwart. Dirt means evidence confirming what we already think we know about them.]

Would you consent to carry a device
that tracked your location in real time
so that your significant other could
locate your position any time they
wanted?

- ~~Yes.~~

✓ No.

Your explanation

This would probably be my greatest nightmare.

Your lover says let us take other lovers. You say to your lover
you have been taken by other lovers. And now your lover is
not your lover is now a lover.

[It is good money, and I am only twenty-one. It feels so free
to be a civilian consultant, to not wear a uniform anymore,
to not shave every day. To put on headphones while I work,
to block out the world with music and not have to worry
about guard duty, or drills, or losing a rifle.]

Would you consider having a serious relationship with someone who works in job that is so secret that they will never be allowed to discuss even the smallest details of it with you?

✓ Yes.

· No.

Your explanation

I'd understand where they're coming from.

.

I leave behind collecting rays that slip through blinds and unsecured curtains of intimacy. I find a surface where everyone is bare by choice, where an algorithm brings us together, not the orange light of a streetlamp.

[The other side becomes more and more paranoid, though paranoia would seem to suggest that they are imagining being haunted, and it is not just their imagination. Intelligence leads to action—when the cell says "wedding" we translate the code to "bombing" and the threat is neutralized. Despite that, members of the cell can't seem to stop saying "wedding."]

This Eros demands mutuality. Show me yours and I'll show you mine. Show me yours slowly.

How much of your true self do you reveal to other people?

✓ I'm an open book.

· I'm about average.

· I'm closed off to most people.

Your explanation

I'm an open book in a foreign language.

[I love to hide in the shadows, to have a tag that lets me into the highest clearance. Out of uniform I begin to feel desirable again, desiring.]

[Despite that signed paper, I tell those intimately close to me which foreign agency the money comes from. It is a name-drop of such huge proportion they do not know what to do. I am too young to really know what this work means, or does, or what this agency has meant for subcontracted violence carried out on others' bodies.]

The soft firmness of the mouth flutters—before a curve, before strands or curls, before deep meeting places where drops of sweat slide slowly. The tongue curls, the teeth ache. If I could collect you in cell by cell, I would. But who can lose the electricity of the inch away, the slow inhale.

Would you like to "live hard, die fast, and leave a beautiful corpse"?

- ~~Yes~~

✓ No

Your explanation

How many beautiful corpses have you seen?

We can be charged bodies attracted and repelled, particles
that are simultaneously here and there. We can hum ourselves to each other, statically. Hydrophilic and suspended
in the sea, lightning connecting through the salt.

[Still, through the surface of excitement some questions infiltrate. The project is supposed to be *objective* surveillance,
but new words start to appear in the reports I translate: Why
change "activist" to "terrorist"? Or "killed" to "murdered"?
The answer is almost too easy, but the questions it brings
up are not.]

Tell the tongue which sensation comes first—skin's roughness, sweat's salt, or heat from the blood beneath. Suddenly
disentangling the sequence becomes paramount. Release is
not a word to ask here.

Do you own any sexy underwear?

- Yes

✓ No

Your explanation

I have one pair of camo underwear. Is that "sexy?"

2014 Update
I have lost the camo underwear. So, no.

[I am not an analyst. I do not sit in the bunker with headphones and listen intently to a source. I am merely a conduit
between a target and interested parties. Unlike the analysts
and their specifically focused target, my station is a meeting point for many intelligence interests. Nuclear weapons,
suicide bombings, a possible airstrike—I am exposed to
everything and therefore know nothing.]

Do you ever date to avoid being alone?

- Yes
- ✓ No

Your explanation

I enjoy being alone. And besides, I'm never truly alone thanks to my imaginary parrot.

I want to believe in the neutrality of distance. Disregard how much air is there, separating my surface from yours. If the body is self-contained then it doesn't matter how close we get. If the body is not self-contained it doesn't matter that I am here and you are there and in between us the-whole-wide-world.

[I imagine analysts who compile reports know their targets as intimately as one human can know another, as intimately as one can know someone without their consent, without that basic intention of language—to be understood.]

[Truth: Saying I was young and I did not know what I was doing is a lie. I knew exactly what I was doing. I could argue my work was mandatory, that my uniformed body was no longer mine, that I had no choice in the matter. But this would also be a lie. By that point the uniform came off and I was doing the same work as before, except for money. Not a lot, but more than most people my age working a shitty postarmy job.]

Are you a "people person"?

- Yes.

✓ No.

Your explanation

I think I'm a person person.

Your lover's new lovers might be perfect plums, easily popped into the mouth in one plump motion. You know that hunger. Your new lovers float like jellyfish on currents you cannot see.

[What I did not know: what this work meant for those characters in the reports. There were dozens of them, possibly hundreds, I cannot remember. And I have no idea anymore how my role in chronicling affected their lives.]

Stomachs hunger for food, substance transformed into the body. Eros hungers for a whole that refuses to become part of itself. Eros cannot conceive of anything greater than the unyielding tug.

Would you be comfortable having a partner whose job requires them to be physically close to very attractive people?

✓ Yes.

· No.

Your explanation

You mean, like librarians?

ACT III: *In Which We Theoretically Reveal Our True Self*

We are not facing when we speak the words *other lovers* to one another. We are side by side looking at a horizon that undresses in front of us—every window a lover's window, every text a doorbell that announces, *Lover, I am here!*

How interested would you be in knowing the details of a partner's sexual history?

✓ Very interested.

· Somewhat interested.

· Not interested.

Your explanation

I'm full of curiosity.

[Though some possible outcomes are not entirely hidden: during my military training the instructors told stories of surveillance targets who met mysterious endings. They related these episodes with a smile—how one morning a target wakes, opens his front door, and walks into a bullet. They told each story as if it was a passive occurrence, as if the target moved toward the bullet and not the other way around. Our instructors framed spying as a game, and it would be a lie to say that the stories did not make me giddy at the thought of playing my part.]

Under the sun we trace a hoop with our arms, a sphere that belongs to us. We say, *Up to here.* We walk the perimeter line tracing the boundary. Inside the shade we log away hours spreading breadcrumbs or birdseed or bait. Each fragment designed to lead the wanderer forward, an irresistible invitation.

[During my training I spent too much time reading the unclassified booklets about weapons used by the surrounding enemy armies. I should have been paying attention to the highly classified abstractions that defined my service. I did so poorly on our weekly tests. It was too hard to resist the glossy pictures that reminded me of childhood world encyclopedias. Too hard to resist the desire to inventory the enemy's intimate objects.]

Do you talk to and or have conversations with yourself, either outloud or in your head?

- Yes, outloud
- ✓ Yes, in my head
- Yes, both
- No, neither

Your explanation

Unless there are cats around, in which case I talk to them.

Pull back your arm, arm your heart, pull the spring on that snap trap. Sharpen your words. Clench your tenses. You know not what you plan to catch, only that catching is the act that matters.

Do you try to draw attention to your body by wearing seductive clothing?

• Yes

✓ No

Your explanation

First I need to know what is this "seductive clothing" you speak of.

[Neither the foreign agency nor the military will admit to hiring me, so the funds are funneled through a temp agency. However, there are laws in place in this country that limit the duration one can work as a temp. After a period of six months the employer must hire the subcontractor directly or terminate them. In order to get around this law, I am terminated, and after a month I am hired back again. In the interim I grow a beard, I buy clothes that might be too tight, and I read.]

I barely remember—two humans sitting facing one another, the splitting of a pomegranate. Each seed tested, the tongue pointing to the most tempting traces. Each chamber a possible vein for the preferred flavor—*Lover, do you like the sour or the sweet?* And the mutual searching for the reddest red, where intensity for the eye promises intensity for the mouth.

Do you have a good imagination?

✓ Yes.

• No.

Your explanation

But I don't always imagine good things.

[After my conscription I stopped reading, though I still carried five books in my backpack wherever I went. I could just never open them. There could be no immersion in another storyline.]

**Hypothetically, do you think you would
be good at being a porn star?**

- Yes

✓ No

Your explanation

But I could probably fix the shower if necessary. Or deliver pizza.

Standing on the edge of a pond, a breeze pushes by and on the other side you see a web move. In it your lover's lovers are tangled, writhing, caught. Your lover watches over, the lovers in a circle, arms to ankles. And on your shore the wind pushes through the gaps in between the strands. An empty music. An idle Eros.

[How is it that taking up a book was only possible after taking off my uniform? Once I allowed those other voices to enter, I couldn't translate in the same way. If I was one of many authors, and the reports were no longer the only text, it meant I was choosing to write them and only them. I would have to take responsibility for the words I facilitated. I know there is a difference between the books I carried and the lives I translated. Certainly, one cannot equate them directly. And yet text is text.]

ACT IV: *In Which We Inventory the Things of the World*

[The symbol of the Israeli Intelligence Corps is a lily. On my shoulder badge the lily was split in half. The left half was green against a white background and the right half was white against a green background, the petals sharp and angular. The colors, I was told, suggest that some things are hidden in plain sight and some can only be seen in hiding. This was repeated to us throughout our training, but I never understood how the symbol was supposed to reveal anything to me.]

Your mouth opens and expecting *I want I want* you're startled to hear *I need I need I need.* Is it you or a lover you plan to adorn with the garlands you collect?

Do you believe in dinosaurs?

✓ Yes

• No

Your explanation

But do dinosaurs believe in me?

In the roughness of an unfamiliar bed, a gust steals the cover and reveals a territory that is not yours, a field of flowers you don't belong to. Are we sliding into our new self, another's frame for us, perhaps a different character entirely? We wish to exchange our shell, to be new again. Instead we find ourselves trapped. In the same, same husk.

[One thing I noticed after enlisting, after putting on a uniform, was a change in my relationship toward want. It was not that I no longer felt desire. That was just as strong as before, possibly stronger. For some reason though, I could no longer allow myself to give in to a desire that existed only in my body. My body belonged to another, not to me. And since my body didn't belong to me I couldn't possibly engage in such selfish desire. Otherwise, if my body did belong to me, how could I possibly explain what my hands were doing, the reports I was writing, the lives I was touching?]

Drawn are all the particles that make us—dander, thread, and dust. Drawn tight, our magnetic core, the air inhaled and exhaled—breaths that stretch from one lover to another, or the light off the arc of our hand as it tilts a glass toward our mouth to taste that last drop.

Is it ever okay to kill another human being?

- ~~Yes.~~

- Yes, to save your own life.

- ~~Yes, if the government orders it.~~

- ✓ Never.

Your explanation

This is an interesting question from an etymological standpoint. One theory is that the word "OK" comes from the American Civil War, when lists of the dead were published in public town squares. "Okay" or "OK" became a shorthand for "O killed," so in that respect, no it is never ok to kill another human being. Now, if the question was "can killing another human being ever be a moral act" I would have to admit that this is beyond the scope of a multiple choice question on a dating website.

[There were rumors that the cooks, with orders from on high, snuck baking soda into the food as a way to reduce sexual appetite and the possibility of desire interfering with work.]

Is love overrated?

- · Yes, absolutely.
- · Yes, a bit.
- · No, it's fine.
- ✓ No, it's underrated.

Your explanation

Maybe romantic love. But love in the broadest sense of human capability to care about others? Definitely underrated.

This Eros sees itself from across the road, leg forever suspended off the curved lip of the curb, about to cross.

[In that time there were so many desires: Desire of the target. Desire of a body that could only be touched by proxy. Desire of an interception of communication. Desire to fall in love with characters and their worlds. Desire of text. Desire of the body. Desire of an ideal that feels all-encompassing— that makes one merge with a whole. That these desires could not easily coexist meant it was easier to let one disappear.]

[I never believed the rumor. For me the decision to embrace self-denial and no lover was only meaningful because I could still feel that ache. It was a choice.]

Can a person change who they are without betraying who they are?

- ~~No, be true to yourself as you are.~~
- ✓ Yes, it's good to evolve
- I'm not sure, but I think about it a lot.
- ~~I don't know, and it's not important.~~

Your explanation

Perhaps not changing would be a betrayal of human nature.

What of your lover in other lovers' beds? Or is this a slip into the old? Should it be a lover in other sheets? A lover's lovers' sheets are diaphanous and made of starlight. Too much? Let's just say they don't have holes like yours.

**What should be done with your
body after you die?**

- ✓ Bury me.
- • Cremate me.
- • By all means, please find a good taxidermist.
- • Something else.

Your explanation

I think I'd like to be buried in the village where I grew up, but I'd be
dead, so it kind of doesn't matter.

At one point the slipping back of a sheet was neither here
nor there. As in, it was everywhere, all the time, forever
a hand in the act of lifting a veil off entwined bodies, the
tendril from which we could be undone.

[So there was no release. With others or alone. I do not know
exactly for how long, but more than thirty months and less
than three years. As long as it felt like my body didn't belong
to me I couldn't let go and drift into desire.]

Do you believe in an afterlife/life after death/resurrection?

- Yes

- No

- ✓ I'm Not Sure

Your explanation

I believe I will eventually find out (or not).

[The act of withholding desire was concurrent with the proliferation of intelligence targets. The more information passed through me, the more undifferentiated the mass of lives and deaths of strangers I could not get close to, the more I felt the need to withhold. To be contained.]

Sitting on the edge of the bed I look over my shoulder at a lover and wonder if we are trapped. Where lies the core that bends us into our orbits, to repeat the same course over and over? This other body could be sleeping deep, or looking up longingly, or even plain bored, and we have been here before, but cannot help retracing the trajectory.

[Sometimes I would push myself to the very edge of desire to see what would happen, how far I could go and still not cross over. *Is this body mine?* Just to make sure I still had an edge.]

Would you take your top off while dancing in a nightclub? (If you're a woman, assume you have a bikini top or bra on underneath)

· Yes

✓ No

Your explanation

I would take it off to use it as a tourniquet in case the person next to me was hemorrhaging. Is that what this question means?

We are left as bodies in a room. The dream that we can cohere like water drops together breaks into a cheap, momentary illusion, and we split off in the end. The other body over our shoulder may reach out to caress our neck, or move a wisp of hair behind our ear. But this is not *we* anymore.

There are exceptions of course, when desire simmers for so long, the vibrations building slowly until every pore, every cell cries out. And so, even when desire boils over, the fire rising so high as to touch the ceiling, even after the storm has crossed the plain, the two bodies still hum at the same frequency, the space between them all sweat and little charged lightning. But these are the exceptions.

[I never broke and gave in to desire. Not until I confessed my secret compact to someone else.]

What is the reason for reaching over and over? Somehow forgetfulness sneaks in between the hinted and the bare. What starts as the curve of a limb or the dimple under the rise of a clavicle slides into an infinity of skin with no traces of an end, just a plane stretching in all directions.

Are military uniforms a turn on?

- • Yes
- ✓ No
- • I wear one to work

Your explanation
I wore them for three years, and they're definitely not a turn on.

[The most limited resource in espionage is attention. Even with the help of AI and its algorithms there are only so many eyes and ears available. The key to spying is learning to pick the most essential targets and within those, the most important utterances. And you can rest assured that if an unknown third party is not collecting your most intimate utterances it is only because you are not important enough.]

[Utterances because, for now at least, we are not able to read minds and so our information always depends on acts of language.]

You and your lover compete to see who has better lovers. You strut on stage dressed in your best feathers, ready to be noticed. When the curtain rises you look over and realize you're alone. Your lover isn't even at the theater. The other seats are empty. The audience is at home, possibly with your lover as new lovers, your lover who is now a lover like any other. You walk out under the marquee and understand that all lovers are simply lovers floating in an undifferentiated sea.

Which is more offensive: book burning or flag burning?

✓ book burning

• ~~flag burning~~

Your explanation

Book flagging

You dream a lover passing by your window will notice your slow drift, a scent revealed that mingles with the night smells of jasmine and pine and wet grass, a scent that captures. You dream of passing by a window, of encountering a reaching out, of a taste so particular and unmistakable.

While walking down the street, you see an amazingly attractive member of your preferred gender. They are completely naked and floating three feet in the air. Which is more intriguing?

- The fact that they're naked
- ✓ The fact that they're defying gravity

Your explanation

Naked people aren't that extraordinary. I'm naked every day.

[Truth: I would have been a terrible analyst. The analyst's most important task is to rule out the redundant, and I still have that inefficient desire for intimacy.]

Is it possible to love someone you don't even like?

✓ Yes

· No

Your explanation

In the broadest definition of love, like, "love thy enemy" kind of love? I would say yes. Romantically, maybe not.

At the end of the night what you find instead is the insistence of a fragrance with all the wrong notes. The eyes can close, but breathing overwhelms with the smell of another.

[The analyst connects the pieces by finding a pattern, a click of one tongue into the curved indentation of another that tells us the piece is in the right place. But there is never a perfect fit.]

We stand in front of a mirror and realize that there is no distinction between I or you or we anymore. Just when we think that we have truly isolated ourselves—the boundary at its most articulated, most solid—we find that our shape is nothing, not alone, not whole, not discrete.

Have you ever gone on a rampant sex spree while depressed, shortly after losing a love?

- Yes
- ✓ No

Your explanation

I went on a spree, but I wasn't depressed (because I went on a spree).

[I would have tried to reconstruct the target's personality from the awkward silences and bad jokes. I would have wanted to know how many toothpicks the target had left, and what kind of music they enjoyed.]

Would you ever record a video of yourself having sex?

✓ Yes

• No

Your explanation

Probably not. Although this one time when I was 12 my karate teacher videotaped us doing karate, and then showed us the video and it remarkably improved my high kicks. So I suppose as long as there was full consent by everyone involved I would consider doing it, just to improve those sexy high kicks.

In a moment a lover looks out to the street, the street looks in, stream of light rendered slow and unpredictable. Bare branches and dead leaves obfuscate one party from another.

[It is my fantasy that the analysts know their targets intimately. Most likely, despite the occasional running joke about Target X's internet porn proclivities, those details do not matter. It is not who the targets are that is important, but what they do—how close they are to completing the bomb, or the nuclear reactor, or to calling the strike.]

Do you think it is acceptable for a person to stand naked in their own window so that people outside can see them?

✓ Yes.

• No.

• ~~It depends on what they look like.~~

• I'm not sure.

Your explanation

As long as they are doing something benign, like eating Chex Mix.

[I eventually leave the project. Perhaps not out of a moral complication. I save enough money and depart the country. Perhaps out of a desire for adventure—the result is still no more reports for me. My position is taken over by others who have similar training. Whether they desire in the same way as me I have no way to know. They too will someday be replaced.]

Your lover strikes with words that have no end, a stream of speaking. You steel yourself, letting the voice drown. The voice stays. How does a lover stay?

[I do know that the work maintained the integrity of some bodies while compromising that of others. This division of whose body deserved to be preserved was based on a distinction of who belongs to us and who belongs to them—a fact which I'll admit at first made the work easier. That both sides seemed intent on harming each other made my actions clearer for a time. I knew which side I was on and whom I had to work with in order to prevent harm or cause it.]

Would you ever sleep with a serial killer?

- ~~Yes~~
- ✓ No

Your explanation

No, but I would sleep with a serial thriller.

Despite the urge to hide wrinkles and blemishes and unwanted hairs, lovers look lovelier from up close, when each eye sees separately, simultaneously. My lover your lover our lover.

Are tears arousing?

✓ Yes

• No

Your explanation

They can be, in the sense that they can reveal a vulnerability, and
that can then be an intimate moment, and therefore also
arousing.

Start with the beginning: when your lover took on other
lovers. Intercept all traces of belonging: when a lover took
on lovers. Complicate the story: when the lover took your
lovers. Delete the redundancies: a lover a lover a lover a
lover a lover.

[I desire again after leaving the country. Crashing on a
friend's spare mattress in this other city and feigning sleep I
make sure the top sheet is pulled just low enough to reveal
a stretch of my back for her to see.]

In another life this Eros would be the splitting of an orange, segments handed around and shared—the seeds planted deep for future trees, for future lovers to enjoy.

How do you think your sex drive compares to what is typical for other people of your age and gender?

- My sex drive is higher than average.
- ✓ My sex drive is about average.
- My sex drive is below average.
- I'm insatiable.

Your explanation

Everyone on this website seems to say that their sex drive is "higher than average," which means, mathematically speaking, that it's actually just average.

[The struggle may be to always narrow down information, to drown out the noise, but the information of a compromised source is useless. The most important act in intelligence is to never reveal your source. Intelligence is valuable only as long as the utterance remains innocent (though the target may not be innocent—people lie to each other all the time). Once the target knows they are being listened to, that their communications are reaching an unintended audience, that information can never be trusted.]

On our devices we wander into the street without looking left or right, while remaining unaware that in truth the web is much larger, extends beyond our little network.

Love without pain is like food without flavor.

✓ True

• False

Your explanation

Eros the Bittersweet

[Our point of access depends exactly on that human weakness, that there are acts we cannot do by ourselves, and that these acts are many, and that while the mind is inaccessible, acts of language, even if whispered at the lowest register, even if encrypted, are always a little bit exposed. We have to go through so many layers in order to touch.]

ACKNOWLEDGMENTS & NOTES

Many thanks to the editors and staff of journals in which parts of this book first appeared:

Gulf Coast: "Wouldn't It"; "Love Drones" (winner of the 2014 *Gulf Coast* Nonfiction
    Prize, judged by John D'Agata)

Passages North: "Fragment | Fragment" (honorable mention for the 2017 *Passages
North* Ray Ventre Nonfiction Prize, judged by Jenny Boully)

Some lines borrowed from: Eric Renner, *Pinhole Photography: From Historic Technique to Digital Application*; Thalia Field, interview in the *Seneca Review*; Raya Morag, "The Living Body and the Corpse—Israeli Documentary Cinema and the *Intifadah*"; Wallace Stevens, "Study of Two Pears"; David Young, "Poem for Adlai Stevenson and Yellow Jackets"; Nurit Stadler, "Terror, Corpse Symbolism, and Taboo Violation: The 'Haredi Disaster Victim Identification Team in Israel' (Zaka)."

My deepest gratitude to the Sarabande staff for seeing this through: Emma Aprile, Joanna Englert, Danika Isdahl, Kristen Miller, Alban Fischer for the maverick design magic, and especially my editor Sarah Gorham who saw the book inside the manuscript.

The writing of this book was supported in part by fellowships from the Fulbright Program, the Taft-Nicholson Center, and the University of Utah.

My deep appreciation to Jenny Boully, Lidia Yuknavitch, Douglas Kearney, and Nicole Walker for their guidance and words on this text when it was nothing but rough edges.

To the writing communities at Brown University, the University of Arizona, and the University of Utah—this book wouldn't have been possible without the conversations we've had, the conversations we're having right now.

Friends, your patience and support gave me the strength to do this. Shout-outs to: Adi Gold, Li Zhen Wang, Doreen Wang, Lindsey Gaydos, Rona Luo, Liat Berdugo, Justin Yampolsky, Craig Reinbold, Tessa Fontaine, and Michelle Macfarlane.

To my teachers, Catherine Imbriglio, Thalia Field, and Paisley Rekdal—you opened the door and showed me what's possible.

A special natural 20 thank you to Ander Monson for being a teacher and a friend, and for DM-ing this entire project behind the scenes for nearly a decade. I wish upon all writers an advocate and mentor as wise and supportive, who can design a book-themed tattoo with one hand while calmly vanquishing all wandering book-monsters with the other. Thank you for being there from the start and for seeing it through to the end.

To Cori A. Winrock—I can't possibly find enough words to show my gratitude for the camaraderie over the past two years, for you breathing and living every word of this book right along with me (often remembering my own words better than I could), for helping me pull back when I was too close and zoom in when I was too removed, for being ruthless with my prose-writer tendencies (and my comma traumas) and heart-making when I couldn't find the hope. I mean it when I say I couldn't have done this without you. Can I send you one more section to look at?

And finally, thank you for the love and support of my family, who seemed to know what I was doing even when I had no idea what I was doing: Margie, Hagi, Tal, Roie, Ariel, Natan, Michael, Saba Egon, Savta Esther, Saba Yisrael, Savta Helen, Saba Emanuel, and all of the aunts and uncles and cousins—you made this fabric, you made this life.

NOAM DORR's work has appeared or is forthcoming in *Gulf Coast, Seneca Review, Wag's Revue, Passages North,* and other places. His essay "Love Drones" won the *Gulf Coast* Nonfiction Prize and was a Notable Essay in *The Best American Essays 2016.* Born and raised in Kibbutz Givat Haim Ichud, Israel, he is a former Fulbright Scholar. He received his MFA in Creative Writing from the University of Arizona, and is currently a doctoral candidate in the Literature and Creative Writing Ph.D. program at the University of Utah.

SARABANDE BOOKS is a nonprofit literary press located in Louisville, KY. Founded in 1994 to champion poetry, short fiction, and essay, we are committed to creating lasting editions that honor exceptional writing. For more information, please visit sarabandebooks.org.